Free Trade Area in Asia

Dr. Ramesh Chand (born 1956) is currently Acting Director and Principal Economist at National Centre for Agricultural Economics and Policy Research, New Delhi. Till recently he was Professor and Head – Agricultural Economics Unit at Institute of Economic Growth, Delhi. He has worked earlier as Professor of Marketing at Punjab Agricultural University, Ludhiana. He was Visiting Professor at University of Wollongong, NSW Australia (2000) and Visiting Fellow at Institute of Developing Economies, Chiba Shi, Japan (2003). His Ph.D. thesis, submitted to Indian Agricultural Research Institute, New Delhi, was selected for Jawaharlal Nehru Award of Indian Council of Agricultural Research in recognition of its outstanding Research contributions. Dr. Chand has worked as consultant for FAO, ESCAP, OECD, World Bank, Indian Institute of Foreign Trade, Delhi and Government of Punjab. At present he is engaged in research on Trade Liberalisation, WTO and Asian Agriculture, Food Policy and Development Economics. Dr. Chand is author of five books and 60 research papers published in reputed national and international journals.

Free Trade Area in Asia

Ramesh Chand

ACADEMIC FOUNDATION
NEW DELHI

First Published in 2006 by
ACADEMIC FOUNDATION
4772-73 / 23 Bharat Ram Road,
(23 Ansari Road), Darya Ganj,
New Delhi - 110 002. INDIA.

Phones : 23245001, 02, 03, 04.
Fax : 011-23245005
e-mail : academic@vsnl.com
www : academicfoundation.com

Free Trade Area in Asia
by Ramesh Chand
ISBN 81-7188-422-9

Designed and typeset by Italics India, New Delhi.
Printed and bound in India.

Contents

Preface 7

Abbreviations 11

1. Background 13

2. Method and Material 25

3. Changing Pattern of Asia's Trade 33

4. Countrywise Trade Trends 49

5. Implications of Emerging Trade Trends in Asia 67

6. Main Findings and Suggestions for a Regional Strategic Framework for Trade in Asia 87

7. Regional Trading Agreements and India 101

Bibliography 119

Index 125

Preface

WORLD has seen renewed interest and surge in preferential trading agreements (PTAs) since 1990. Initially it was believed that the turn towards regionalism in trade was due to failure of global community to provide effective mechanism for multilateral trade liberalisation as seen in obstacles in pre-Uruguay round GATT negotiations. However, number of PTAs have proliferated after multilateral trade accord was concluded and its implementation began under the auspices of WTO in 1995. Countries like USA which were staunch supporter of multilateralism and strongly opposed regionalism in trade started taking active interest in creating trade blocs and PTAs, not only in the region of proximity but even with the countries located at very far off places in other continents. This has changed the nature of trading arrangement from regional trading agreements to preferential trading agreements reflecting more the preferences or strategic interest than the geographic factors.

These trends in regionalism are causing externality to outsiders. Various countries, not already part of regional arrangement, are forced to go for PTAs to counter the adverse impact of other PTAs on them. More stronger motivation for PTA, especially RTA, is provided by internal factors i.e. opportunity for trade creation as a result of rationalisation of tariff and specialisation that follow trade liberalisation and harmonisation of policies among members of RTAs. The present study has looked at the internal factors in the case of Asian countries to go for regional integration in trade. The study also analyses implications of RTA in Asia on regional and global welfare. Finally, strategic framework for regional integration in trade to counter the effect of external factors and to take advantage of emerging trade opportunities within Asia is proposed.

This has been accomplished by analysing various aspects of intra and extra Asia trade, inter country trade, and world trade during the period after 1990 in which almost all countries liberalised trade to various extent and also initiated some domestic policy reforms either on their own or to meet commitments under Uruguay round General Agreement on Trade and Tariffs. The study also analysed implications of RTA in Asia on regional and global welfare. Finally, it proposes strategic framework for regional integration in trade to counter the effect of external factors and to take advantage of emerging trade opportunities within Asia. A postscript chapter has been added to the book to provide an overview of India's engagement with Preferential Trading Arrangements.

The study is the outcome of research carried out by me as Visiting Research Fellow, at Institute of Developing Economies, Chiba Shi, Japan. I am extremely grateful to

IDE and JETRO (Japan External Trade Organisation) for inviting me and for providing financial support to carry out this study. I am equally thankful to Institute of Economic Growth, in particular to Professor B.B. Bhattacharya, for granting me leave to work at IDE. I owe special debt to Shuji Uchikawa who helped me in numerous ways during my stay in IDE. He took care of various problems which a foreign scholar faces in Japan and guided and helped me at every step. Mr. Kensuke Kubo provided me wonderful company which made my stay at IDE enjoyable and memorable. I appreciate staff of IDE library for their prompt help in arranging various publications needed by me. I am grateful to the staff of International Exchange Division, in particular to Yuzuro Moriwaki, Rumiko Sasajima and to Tsutomu Ashutomi for logistic support. Finally, I would like to express my gratitude to Dr. S. Hirashima who encouraged me and supported me in several ways to visit IDE to undertake this work.

Ramesh Chand

New Delhi

Abbreviations

AFTA	ASEAN Free Trade Area
ASEAN	Association of South East Asian Nations
BIMST-EC	Bangladesh-India-Sri Lanka-Thailand Economic Cooperation
CECA	India-Singapore Comprehensive Economic Cooperation Agreement
DAC	Developing Asian Countries
EHP	Early Harvest Programme
ESCAP	Economic and Social Commission for Asia and the Pacific
EU	European Union
FTA	Free Trade Area (Agreement)
GATT	General Agreement on Trade and Tariff
GSTP	Global System of Trade Preferences
LDC	Least Developed Countries

MFN	Most Favoured Nations
NAFTA	North America Free Trade Area
OA	Outside Asia
OECD	Organisation for Economic Cooperation and Development
PTA	Preferential Trading Arrangement/ Agreement/Area
ROW	Rest of the World
RTA	Regional Trading Arrangement (Area)
SAARC	South Asian Association for Regional Cooperation
SACU	Southern African Customs Union
SAFTA	South Asia Free Trade Area
SAPTA	SAARC Preferential Trading Agreement
TE	Triennium Ending
USA	United States of America
WTO	World Trade Organisation

1

Background

THE decade of the 1990s and the early years of twenty first century have witnessed profound changes in the international economic environment. The period has been marked by a sharp growth in the number of regional trading agreements and the implementation of the multi-lateral Uruguay round General Agreement on Trade and Tariff under the auspices of the World Trade Organisation (WTO). This has created a piquant situation for several WTO member countries. On the one hand, there is a WTO move towards multi-lateral liberalisation, based on the principle of most favoured nations, requiring member countries to open up and liberalise their economies by reducing trade barriers and to undertake policy reforms to remove market and trade distortions. On the other hand, more and more countries are opting for various sorts of trading agreements that provide preferential access to the members and discriminate against non- members. This helps not only in a general trade promotion among the countries that constitute trading blocs but also helps to create protection against outside members while liberalising on a selective basis. Conversely, this puts the other countries, not part of the trading bloc, in a disadvantageous position in terms of access to the markets of countries operating in a Preferential Trade Area (PTA) *vis à vis* the countries within the PTA. Also the countries that do not form part of the trading bloc are unable to go in for selective liberalisation with some countries, if this is perceived to be beneficial, without allowing such liberalisation to all the countries. These seem to be the compelling reasons for proliferation of preferential trading agreements since the early 1990s when serious moves towards multilateral trade liberalisation were initiated and later institutionalised through formation of the WTO.

While there has been a strong trend towards regional and preferential trade agreements in the world, Asian countries have opted for unilateral liberalisation on an MFN basis. Except for a sub regional approach (Free trade area of ASEAN) in East and South East Asia the region did not have any effective and large preferential trade blocs. This has placed the Asian countries in a sort of disadvantageous position when facing the global competitive liberalisation that has accelerated since the early 1990s. This also raises several questions for example: Why is there a growth in regionalism when almost all the countries are committed to multilateralism through the WTO? Is regionalism in trade blocs going to stay and pose more serious challenges to the countries outside region? What are the undercurrents in regionalism in other continents? Why has a larger regional trade group in Asia not been formed? Is it because a neighbourhood advantage did not exist in Asia? Is the trade pattern in Asia evolving towards regional concentration and what are its implications? This study is an attempt to address such questions. The questions relating to growth, rationale and future of regionalism are discussed in this chapter while other questions of an empirical nature are taken up in the subsequent chapters.

1.1 Rationale and Motivation for Regionalism

There have been various motivations for the formation of regional or preferential trade agreements. Traditionally, the motivations have been: (1) to increase market access and to promote the gains from trade occurring as a result of rationalisation and specialisation; (2) to enhance political cohesion; and (3) to further other trade and economic policy goals (OECD 1993). It was widely perceived that regional integration provides opportunities to exploit economies of scale and specialisation to promote long run growth. This type of argument formed the main basis for the rise of regionalism during the 1960s and 1970s. This trend in regionalism, which is also termed as first regionalism or old regionalism, did not go very far in involving developing countries in RTAs and PTAs. By beginning of 1980s all attempts are said to have suffered reversals to a greater or smaller extent (Axline 1994, p.4).

A new wave of regionalism started during late 1980s which was different than the earlier trend of the 1960s and 1970s. The main driving force for the new regionalism or second regionalism, *a la* Bhagwati, is said to be the distinct change in U.S. policy to follow a regional path in a complete reversal of its earlier policy of key defender of multilateralism (Bhagwati 1994). Initially it appeared as if failure to successfully negotiate multi lateral trade agreements lead to the emergence of regional groupings but subsequent events show that regionalism has grown very fast after the successful multilateral Uruguay round in 1994. According to the information at WTO site the number of RTAs has grown from 31 in 1990 to 80 in 1995 and 184 in March 2003 (also see Fig 1.1). These numbers indicate an explosion of Regional Integration agreements after the WTO set up in 1995.

It has been rightly noted by some scholars that the old regionalism was to a large extent motivated by a desire to substitute for insufficient multilateralism and/or to facilitate multilaterism whereas the new regionalism has emerged as a consequence of post multilateral success (Ethier 1998). Economic globalism and its challenges are seen as the major forces behind the growing acceptability and expansion of economic regionalism across the world (Khan and Khan 2003).

FIGURE 1.1

RTAs in Force by Date of Entry into Force

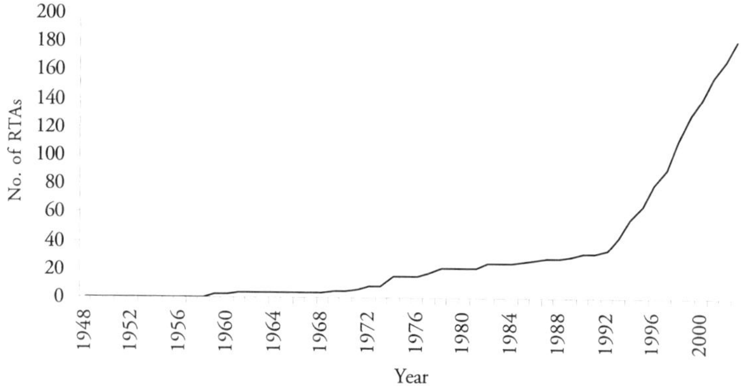

1.2 WTO, Multilateralism and Future of RTAs

Formation of RTAs allowing preferential access to RTA members and discriminating against non members as such appears to be a violation of GATT or the WTO principle of equal treatment for all trading partners (most favoured nation). The MFN clause reads:

> ...any advantage, favour, privilege or immunity granted by any contracting party to any product originating in or destined for any other country shall be accorded immediately and unconditionally to the like product originating in or destined for the territories of all other contracting parties.

However, three WTO articles provide derogation from this principle. These are: (a) Article XXIV of GATT; (b) Article V of the General agreement on Trade in Services; and (c) the Enabling Clause. Primary provisions for RTAs and Free Trade Areas and Custom Union are contained in Article XXIV which states that if a Free Trade Area or Custom Union is created, duties and other trade barriers should be reduced or removed on substantially all sectors of trade in the group. Non members should not find trade with the group more restrictive than before the group was set up.[1] The PTAs that sprang up in the post WTO period have unexpectedly involved freer trade but not free trade.

---

1. *As reported by WTO, see* wto.org/English/thewto_e/whatis_e/tif_e/bey3_e.htm *updated 30.4.2003. There is some difference in respect of reduction in tariff barriers. According to Panagariya and Srinivasan (1998), Article XXIV gave a legal status to Free Trade Area and Custom Union by allowing contacting parties to form such arrangements provided they eliminate rather than just lower trade barriers. Thus, according to them a Preferential Trading Agreement that involves only partial liberalisation among members is ruled out.*

Secondly, in most of the cases several items are excluded from a reduction in trade barriers. Thirdly, PTAs are being finalised between/ among countries not falling in the same region but located even in distant places, even different continents.

There is no consensus on whether the growing number of RTAs promotes multilateral liberalisation or hinders it. This has been termed as the "building blocs or stumbling block" debate and a recent review is provided by Panagariya (1999). Those who view the RTA as promoting trade liberalisation argue that the RTA provides a quicker route to trade liberalisation, as the like minded group of a small number of countries find it easy to negotiate and reach a consensus. PTAs are also said to be helpful in achieving substantial reductions in barriers to trade in difficult areas like agriculture. But there are counter arguments also.

Notwithstanding the debate on the favourable or adverse impact of RTAs on multi-lateral liberalisation there is a feeling that RTAs are now a fact of international economic order and they are going to be there irrespective of progress in multilateralism. Second, according to Bhagwati (1994), who is a strong opponent of RTAs and a staunch supporter of multilateralism for promoting global welfare, *"careful analysis of the causes of the resurrection of regionalism suggests that regionalism this time is likely to endure."*

1.3 Strategic Implications for Non Members (Asia)

The current spate of regionalism has some strategic implications for forging a regional trading bloc in Asia. Even if there is no conviction about the positive role of trading blocs for multi-lateral trade liberalisation the need for a trading bloc exists for several reasons. One, if the formation of the trading bloc improves welfare. Two, to counter the adverse impact of an explosion in the number of RTAs around the world. Three, to provide a powerful supra RTA to obliterate the need for bilateral and sub regional RTAs which are likely to create problems in terms of trade deflections, spaghetti bowl and preferential trade agreement with countries from the outside region.

It is somewhat ironical that there is no serious move in Asia to go ahead and establish a strong and genuine free trade area covering the large region despite GATT and WTO rules being biased toward regional trade arrangements. Though there are two agreements in this direction at the sub regional level, namely, the ASEAN agreement in South East Asia and the SAARC agreement in South Asia, they have not achieved much. The ASEAN agreement was initially concerned with food security and contains a provision for sharing rice stock in times of food shortages. Subsequently, AFTA was formed within ASEAN to liberalise regional trade but it has also not achieved much in terms of freeing agriculture trade. The South Asian Free Trade Agreement (SAFTA) under SAARC has been marred by political conflicts between India and Pakistan.

1.4 Exploring the Possibilities and Implications of Asian Trading Bloc

In general there has been a more than proportionate trade among neighbours than with other countries. What could be the reason for this? According to Krugman (1991) the strong tendency towards neighbourhood trade clearly shows that distance still matters and creates natural trading advantages. Some other researchers also found a strong linkage between bilateral trade and proximity factors like distance, adjacency and cultural similarities (Frankel and Wei 1996, 1997; Engel and Rogers 1997; Deardorf and Stern 1994). However, Bhagwati (1992) and Panagariya (1995) argued that the concentration observed in neighbourhood trade is the result of a discriminatory and preferential trading arrangement and they rejected the importance of geographic proximity.

Apart from the tendency towards a concentration of trade among neighbouring countries, it has also been observed that trade continues to grow at a faster rate among neighbouring countries than with others. This is hard to explain in terms of factors like geographic proximity. One can expect more or disproportionate trade among neighbours due to factors like proximity, cultural similarity, and better communication. However, disproportionate growth in trade within a region compared to that with other regions cannot be explained by neighbourhood and such variables because they do not change with time. One explanation for a disproportionate growth in regional trade is that policy regimes followed by neighbouring countries at similar stages of development also tend towards similarity. To the extent that neighbourhood characteristics encourage trade, liberalisation should encourage growth in the share of neighbourhood trade in total trade. Since liberalisation occurs in stages, trade patterns display a dynamic where growth in intra regional trade exceeds the growth in inter regional trade (Diao, Roe and Somwaru 1999). These scholars argued that if this pattern occurs, then regional trade arrangements may be entered into to further remove obstacles to trade and to avert policy reversals. This study would examine whether this kind of evolution is taking place in Asia to forge regional trade arrangements.

The second rather more important aspect relating to the Regional Trade Agreement (RTA) is its impact on the welfare of members of the RTA and non member countries. Krugman (1995) shows that, in principle, Free Trade Areas are welfare enhancing. The impact of Regional Trade Agreements (RTA) on welfare is generally seen by examining trade creation and trade diversion within the region and outside the region. Trade creation occurs when some domestic production in a nation is replaced by a lower cost import from another member nation. This is reflected in the growth of intra regional trade. This increases the welfare of the member nations as it leads to greater specialisation in production based on comparative advantage. On the other hand, trade diversion occurs when lower cost imports from outside the region (having RTA) are replaced by higher cost import from a nation within the RTA because of preferential treatment to members of the RTA. Trade diversion by itself reduces welfare because it shifts resources away from the comparative advantage. This can cause a positive or negative impact on the welfare of the members but it reduces the welfare of non members (Salvitore 1990, ch.10). The present study seeks to examine the potential welfare effect of regional integration in Asia using an *ex ante* approach.

As mentioned above, growth in intra regional trade *vis à vis* inter regional trade provides a useful guide to the period preceding the regional trade integration arrangement to promote trade liberalisation. Several countries in Asia started some sort of trade liberalisation in the early 1990s while implementation of the Uruguay Round Agreement

(URA) led to further liberalisation of trade policies and reforms in domestic policies. Has this liberalisation affected the regional pattern in agricultural trade? If yes, what is the direction of change and what are its implications for further liberalisation, policy action and welfare? Can this information be used as a guide to analyse the prospects of regional integration in trade and to understand its potential benefits? This study would address such issues.

1.5 Objectives and Hypotheses

It is hypothesised that there is lot of potential opportunity for the growth of intra Asian trade if the countries open up trade to one another. This can be tested by looking at the growth rate in intra regional trade during the 1990s when almost all Asian countries followed some sort of trade liberalisation. The second hypothesis is that free trade in Asia would enhance welfare for Asia and also for the rest of the World. The third hypothesis is that due to the importance of the agriculture sector in Developing Asian Countries, the liberalisation of agriculture trade can provide a stimulus to regional concentration and regional agreement for relatively free trade.

Objectives

1. To study the effect of the trade liberalisation of the 1990s on intra regional agricultural and non-agricultural trade in Asia *vis à vis* extra Asia and world trade.
2. To estimate changes in the regional concentration of agricultural and non-agricultural trade in Asia during the 1990s and to analyse its implications for future liberalisation of trade.

3. To examine the propensity of an Asian country to trade within Asia and outside Asia.
4. To undertake an *ex ante* analysis of regional trade in agriculture and non-agriculture on trade growth, trade creation and diversion.
5. To analyse the prospects for a regional integration in Asia and to propose a strategy for implementing regional strategic framework for trade liberalisation in Asia.

1.6 Organisation of the Study

Following the Introduction, the study is organised into five chapters. Chapter 2 describes the sources of data and analytical tools used in the study. Chapter 3 undertakes an analysis of patterns in intra and extra Asia trade during the 1990s and examines the growth rate in total and agricultural trade in Asia and the rest of the World. Changing contours of trade between Japan and Developing Asian Countries (DAC) are also analysed in this chapter. The fourth chapter discusses trade performance and trade trends for the major economies of Asia. Implications of the emerging trade pattern in Asia for the welfare of Asian countries and rest of the world and for formation of Regional Trading Arrangement (RTA) in Asia are discussed in detail in the fifth chapter. The sixth chapter presents the conclusion of the study and suggests a strategic framework for regional integration in Asia. The last chapter was included in the volume at a later stage to provide an overview of India's engagements in RTAs.

2

Method and Material

THE study uses data from cross trade tables of the United Nations International Trade Statistics Yearbook for the period 1980 to 2000. Country level data on the direction of trade for major economies in Asia was used from the IMF publications such as Direction of Trade Statistics Yearbook, to examine the trend and share in trade with one another, as also with Asia and rest of the World. Data on some other aspects was obtained from the World Bank publication on World Development Indicators and Asian Development Bank publications on Key Indicators, the UNCTAD publication on the Handbook of Statistics, and the United Nations Publications on National Accounts and Industrial Production and Statistical Yearbook.

The analysis covers Japan and other Asian countries classified in the category of 'Other Asia' or `Developing Asia.' It does not include the Central Asian Republics and Middle East part of the Asian continent. Except for Japan the group of other countries in this study is termed as Developing Asian Countries (DAC). It includes Bangladesh, Cambodia, China mainland, China Hongkong, Taiwan province of China, India, Indonesia, Korea (South), Lao, Malaysia, Mangolia, Myanmar, Nepal, Pakistan, Singapore, Sri Lanka, Thailand, and Vietnam and other small and island countries in the region.

The study uses the trend, growth and decomposition approach as followed by Diao, Roe and Somwaru (1999). It states that if a regional trade agreement is formed, in order to secure and enhance mutual benefits from the intra regional growth in trade, then the trade series should reveal a discernible change in intra versus inter (extra) regional trade prior to the formation of the RTA. We have attempted to examine these features for the developing Asia region and for whole of Asia including Japan.

While the pattern in the intra and inter regional trade share provides a preliminary assessment of the potential for designing a Regional Integration Agreement, these measures do not correctly reveal the existence of a regional bias (concentration in trade). In other words, shares of intra regional trade in a region's total trade are considered to be an inadequate indicator of a regional bias induced by preferential policy on the part of members in the region (Anderson and Norheim 1994). This is particularly true if trade shares are used at a point of time in a static sense or if some country in the region gets divided or united to give rise to more/lesser number of countries.

The above limitation does not apply if the inference about an increase or decrease in regionalisation is drawn by looking at the changes in shares of intra and extra regional trade over time provided the members in the regions remain the same i.e. there is no change in the geography of each member country due to the division of any country or reorganisation of its borders. In the case of developing Asia there has not been any change in the geography of member countries during the study period that could influence the regional share in trade. However, an increase in intra regional trade share or a higher growth in intra regional trade compared to extra regional trade in itself does not prove the existence of a regional bias or a regional concentration of trade. To establish a regional bias in trade one needs to prove whether countries in a region or group are trading proportionately more among themselves relative to the outside world. This is accomplished by estimating an Intensity Index for intra regional trade and Intensity index for extra regional trade.

The intensity index for intra regional trade is roughly the ratio of share of regional trade remaining in the region to the share of the region in world trade. If there is no regional concentration of trade then the intensity index is one. The value of index being more than 1 for intra regional trade is evidence of a regional bias in trade and an intensity index of less than 1 for extra regional trade is evidence of a bias against the outside region. Trade intensity measures are found to reveal a regional bias in the distribution of trade more accurately (dell' Aquila *et al.* 1995). Intensity index developed by Kojima (1964) and extensively used by Anderson and Norheim (1993) for intra regional and extra regional trade are given below. Further, we have distinguished three situations. One, the index for country i to region j which includes i. Two, the index for country k to region j which does not include country k. Three, for the region itself comprising 'n' number of countries.

a. Trade Intensity Index for Intra Regional Import

For country i's import from country j:

$$\frac{\text{(Import by i from j / Total import by i)}}{\text{(Total export from j } \textit{less} \text{ export to i) / (World export } \textit{less} \text{ export from i)}}$$

For country k's import from j:

$$\frac{\text{(Import by k from j / Total import by k)}}{\text{(Total export from j) / (World export } \textit{less} \text{ export from k)}}$$

Since k is not a part of the region j there is no need to subtract its export from the total export from j. This formula was followed to compute Intensity of trade between Japan and group of Developing Asian Countries (DAC).

For region as a whole - for import:

$$\frac{\text{(Intra regional import / Total import by j)}}{\text{(Total export from j) / (World export } \textit{less} \text{ average export by a country in region j)}}$$

The average export by a country is taken as the sum of trade by all countries in the region divided by the number of countries in the region.

b. Trade Intensity Index for Intra Regional Export

For country i's import from j:

$$\frac{\text{(Export from i to j / Total export of i)}}{\text{(Total import of j } \textit{less} \text{ import of i) / (World import } \textit{less} \text{ import of i)}}$$

For country k's import from j:

$$\frac{\text{(Export from k to j / Total export from k)}}{\text{(Total import of j) / (World import } \textit{less} \text{ import by k)}}$$

For region as a whole - for export:

$$\frac{\text{(Intra regional export/Total export from the region)}}{\text{(Total import by j)/(World import } \textit{less} \text{ average import by a country in region j)}}$$

Average import by a country is taken as the sum of trade by all countries in the region divided by the number of countries in the region.

c. Trade Intensity Index for Extra Regional Import

For country i's import from outside j:

$$\frac{\text{(Import by i from outside the region/Total import by i)}}{\text{(Total export from outside region)/(World export } \textit{less} \text{ export from i)}}$$

For country k's import from outside j:

$$\frac{\text{(Import by k from outside region /Total import by k)}}{\text{(Total export from the outside region)/(World export } \textit{less} \text{ export from k)}}$$

Since k is not a part of the region j there is no need to subtract its export from the total export from j. This formula was followed to compute Intensity of trade between Japan and DAC.

For region as a whole - for import:

$$\frac{\text{(Extra regional import/Total import from j)}}{\text{(Total export from outside region)/(World export } \textit{less} \text{ average export by a country in region j)}}$$

d. Trade Intensity Index for Extra Regional Export

For country i's export to region outside j:

$$\frac{\text{(Export from i to outside region/Total export from i)}}{\text{(Total import by outside region)/(World import } \textit{less} \text{ import by i)}}$$

For country k's export to outside j:

$$\frac{\text{(Export from k to outside region/Total export from k)}}{\text{(Total import by outside world)/(World import } \textit{less} \text{ import by k)}}$$

For region as a whole - for export:

$$\frac{\text{(Extra regional export/Total export from j)}}{\text{(Total import by outside region)/ (World import } \textit{less} \text{ average import by a country in region j).}}$$

Further, a decline in extra regional IIT over time does not reveal correctly whether the increase in regionalisation of trade is causing a trade diversion for the outside world. The correct measure to find out whether change in a policy that increased regionalisation of trade caused an adverse affect on the region's trade with the outside world is given by Index of Propensity to Trade (IPT). This index is obtained by multiplying IIT by openness to trade (ratio of GDP traded). An increase in propensity to trade indicates trade creation while decrease in propensity to trade indicates trade diversion. Thus, even if the intensity to trade with the outside region falls, due to a change in policy that increases the regional concentration of trade, it may not result in a decline in the propensity to trade if the trade to GDP ratio increases and becomes large enough. The index of propensity to trade (IPT) was computed as under:

e. Propensity to Export Extra Regionally

$= (\Sigma X_{iR}/\Sigma GDP_i)$ * Intensity to export extra regionally

Where,

X_{iR} is export of country i in the region, GDPi is country i's GDP.

f. Propensity to Import Extra Regionally

$= (\Sigma M_{iR} / \Sigma GDP_i)$ * Intensity to import extra regionally

g. Propensity to Export Intra Regionally

$= (\Sigma X_{ir} / GDP_i)$ * Intensity to export intra regionally

h. Propensity to Import Intra Regionally

$= (\Sigma M_{ir} / GDP_i)$ * Intensity to import intra regionally

Propensity to trade extra regionally or intra regionally is taken as an average of the propensity to import and export for the respective group.

3

Changing Pattern of Asia's Trade

ASIA has a unique place in the global economy. Its inhabitants include the world's poorest as also the richest. It has countries like Bangladesh, Nepal, Philippines, Afghanistan, Lao, Vietnam and Cambodia where more than one third of the total population live below the poverty line. On the other end is Japan which has emerged as the second largest economic power in the world in a short span of less than four decades through a miraculous economic growth. There is a tremendous diversity even in respect of trade. Some countries trade more than their GDP like Singapore, Hongkong, Malaysia and Thailand whereas trade in some countries like Myanmar is still in single digit in terms of per cent of GDP. Some countries in Asia have brought about a dramatic improvement in the living standards of their people through trade led growth whereas some other countries till recently had strong apprehensions about the impact of trade on domestic economies.

The decade of the 1990s has seen tremendous change in the attitude of different countries towards trade. There has also been distinctive economic growth in the hitherto laggard Asian economies. This has raised Asia's importance in the global economy to a great extent. Some of these changes can be seen from Table 3.1.

Asia which consists of developing Asian countries (DAC) and Japan accounts for 55 per cent of the world population and one fourth of global GDP. The status of Japan is unique in Asia in particular and in the global economy in general. Japan accounts for 2.1 per cent of the world population and 15.5 per cent of global GDP. In contrast to this, the group of DAC with 53.3 per cent of the world population produces only one tenth of world GDP. It is amazing that Japan with four per cent of the total population of Asia, produces sixty per cent of Asia's goods and services. Thus, the combined GDP of all DAC, including population giants like China and India, is 33 per cent lower than Japan taken as a single country. No wonder, the per capita income in Japan is more than 37 times the average per capita income in DAC. Similarly, the per capita income in DAC is less than one fifth of the average per capita income in the world. However, the position of DAC *vis à vis* World and Japan is now undergoing a significant change with a faster growth in GDP and trade in the developing Asia region. The growth rate in GDP during 1990 to 2001 shows that DAC economies were growing two and half times faster than the global economy and about five times faster than the Japanese economy. The trend growth rate in GDP in DAC economies was 6.2 per cent compared to 2.7 per cent annual growth rate for the World as a whole and 1.3 per cent for Japan. Similarly, DAC trade was growing annually by 8.5 per cent compared to the 6.6 per cent growth rate in world trade and 4.3 per cent in Japanese trade. These growth rates show that output and trade in Asian developing countries was growing at a much faster rate than rest of the World. It is of considerable interest and relevance, to analyse how these changes have affected the trade pattern among DAC and with outside world, for formulating policies and strategies to benefit Asian countries.

TABLE 3.1

Asia in the World Economic Setting

Aspect	Year/ Period	World	Developing Asia	Japan	Developing Asia and Japan
1. Population million	2000	6057	3230 (53.3)	127 (2.1)	3357 (55.4)
2. GDP $ billion	2000	31362	3213 (10.2)	4876 (15.5)	8089 (25.8)
3. Total merchandise trade $ billion	2000	12360	2332 (18.9)	780 (6.3)	3112 (25.2)
4. Per capita GDP US $	2000	5178	995	36622	2410
5. Growth rate in GDP %/year	1990-2001	2.7	6.2	1.3	
6. Growth rate in trade based on trend %/year	1991-2000	6.6	8.5	4.3	

Sources:

1. World Development Indicators, World Bank, 2003.
2. Trade Statistics Yearbook, United Nations.
3. Direction of Trade, IMF, 2003.

3.1 DAC, Japan and World Trade

Basic information on direction of trade in agricultural, non-agricultural and all merchandise products for DAC, Japan and the World as a whole is provided in Table 3.2 for the trienniums ending (TE) 1992, 1995, 1998 and 2000. The table indicates the quantitative dimensions of world trade, import and export between World and DAC, DAC and Japan and World and Japan. Total world merchandise trade was valued at US$ 3531 billion during the early 1990s which increased to $ 5322 billion by TE 1998. There was a further increase to $ 5678 billion by TE 2000. Between TE 1998 and TE 2000 world export to Japan declined by $ 6 billion whereas export from Japan in the same period increased by $ 21 billion. The entire decline in the import of Japan resulted from a decline in the value of agriculture imports; non-agriculture imports show a marginal increase. There was a decline in the recent years in agricultural imports by DAC and the World but this decline was either not big enough to cause a decline in the total imports or was more than offset by an increase in non-agricultural imports unlike the case with Japan.

The total import by DAC increased from 496 billion during TE 1992 to $ 834 billion by TE 1995. The increase turned out to be much smaller during the next six years mainly due to the economic crisis faced by the group of East and South east Asian countries during 1997 to 1999.

Intra DAC trade was estimated at 185 billion during early 1990s which increased to $ 421 billion by the end of twentieth century. Japan's export to DAC or DAC import from Japan increased from 104 billion during TE 1992 to $162 billion by the mid 1990s. After this, DAC imports from Japan stagnated. However, the DAC export to Japan followed a rising trend even during the recent years. Japan had a high level of surplus in trade balance which witnessed

TABLE 3.2

Trade matrix for World, Japan and Developing Asian Countries, 1990-2000

(Unit: $ Billion FOB)

Export to → Export from ↓	Period	Total Trade			Agricultural Trade			Non-agricultural Trade		
	Triennium Ending	World	Japan	DAC	World	Japan	DAC	World	Japan	DAC
World	1992	3531	191	496	488	53	57	3043	138	439
	1995	4383	264	834	575	64	82	3808	200	752
	1998	5322	269	908	656	63	97	4665	206	811
	2000	5678	263	915	617	56	89	5061	207	826
Japan	1992	314	—	104	3.9	—	2.5	310	—	101
	1995	400	—	162	4.7	—	3.3	395	—	159
	1998	407	—	164	5.1	—	3.7	402	—	161
	2000	428	—	163	5.2	—	3.6	423	—	159
DAC	1992	518	68	185	64	16	23	454	52	163
	1995	789	97	309	85	20	34	703	77	275
	1998	1012	117	401	95	20	40	916	97	361
	2000	1109	124	421	87	18	36	1021	107	385

Source: United Nations Trade Statistics Yearbook, various issues.

further increase during the recent years. It also had a surplus in trade with Developing Asian Countries but the magnitude of surplus followed a sharp decline after the mid 1990s.

3.2 Growth Rate in Intra and Extra Asia and World Trade

As mentioned earlier, DAC trade witnessed a faster growth than world trade during the 1990s. Further, there are two dimensions of trade in the regional context i.e. trade within the region (intra regional) and trade outside the region (extra regional). The growth rate in the two types of trade helps in identifying the partners or the region where faster or where slower growth is taking place. This information for total, agricultural and non-agricultural trade is provided in Table 3.3 for DAC and the World, in Table 3.4 for World and Asia including DAC and Japan and in Table 3.5 for Japan's trade with DAC and rest of the World.

During 1991 to 2000 world trade in agricultural products witnessed an annual trend growth rate of 3.20 per cent while non-agricultural products increased annually by 7.11 per cent. The growth rate in trade in the two types of products in the DAC group was 4.73 and 8.92 per cent, respectively, which was well above the growth rate in world trade. In the same period, the DAC export of non-agricultural products increased at the rate of 10.42 per cent which was higher than the growth in non-agricultural imports. The situation was just the reverse in the case of agricultural products whose imports increased at a much higher rate (5.79 per cent) compared to the growth rate in exports which was 3.70 per cent. Thus, agricultural and non-agricultural products were showing different types of trade trends. In the case of total products, exports were growing by 9.75 per cent annually compared to a 7.15 per cent growth rate in imports.

TABLE 3.3

Growth Rates in Intra and Extra Asia and World Trade

(per cent per year)

Aspect	Import			Export			Total Trade	
	Intra DAC	Extra DAC	Total	Intra DAC	Extra DAC	Total	Developing Asia	World
Total	10.33	4.95	7.15	10.33	9.40	9.75	8.50	6.63
Agricultural	5.67	5.87	5.79	5.67	2.48	3.70	4.73	3.20
Non-agricultural	10.85	4.86	7.31	10.85	10.06	10.42	8.92	7.11

Note: DAC – Developing Asian Countries.

Source: United Nations Trade Statistics Yearbook, various issues.

TABLE 3.4

Growth Rates in Intra and Extra Asia (including Japan) and World Trade

(per cent per year)

Aspect	Import			Export			Total Trade	
	Intra Asia	Extra Asia	Total	Intra Asia	Extra Asia	Total	Asia	World
Total	8.47	3.82	6.40	8.47	7.05	7.70	7.11	6.63
Agricultural	3.67	3.43	3.53	3.69	3.72	3.70	3.59	3.20
Non - agricultural	8.98	3.95	6.87	8.98	7.22	8.08	7.51	7.11

Source: United Nations Trade Statistics Yearbook, various issues.

TABLE 3.5

Growth Rates in Japan's Trade with DAC and Rest of the World

(per cent per year)

	Japan's Import from		Japan's Export to		DAC Import from		DAC Export to	
	DAC	ROW	DAC	ROW	Japan	Outside Asia	Japan	Outside Asia
Total	8.00	1.42	4.91	2.70	4.91	7.70	8.00	9.99
Agricultural	0.30	0.69	4.08	1.87	4.08	5.87	0.30	4.73
Non - agricultural	9.83	1.76	4.95	2.71	4.95	7.96	9.83	10.49

Note: DAC – Developing Asian Countries

ROW – Rest of the World

Source: United Nations Trade Statistics Yearbook, various issues.

Dividing the export and import from developing Asian countries in intra and extra DAC categories shows the presence of strong patterns. Trade among DAC economies increased annually by more than 10 per cent during 1991 to 2000. The growth rate in intra DAC exports was about 1 percentage point higher than the extra DAC export but import among DAC increased by more than double the rate of growth in import from rest of the World. A faster growth in intra DAC import compared to extra DAC import is due to non-agricultural products; agricultural products show a slightly lower growth in intra DAC imports compared to extra DAC imports. In the case of exports, intra DAC trade in non-agricultural products was increasing only at a slightly higher rate than extra DAC trade but intra DAC export of agricultural products followed more than double the growth rate in extra DAC exports. In other words, for non-agricultural products, intra Asia imports were rising at a much faster rate than extra Asia imports and for agricultural products intra Asia exports were rising at a much faster rate than extra Asia exports. From this it can be inferred that the demand for Asian products was expanding much faster in Asia than in rest of the World.

In Asia, Japan is a very big economy and a highly developed country but it has been suffering from economic stagnation for a long period whereas the rest of Asia (as a group of Developing Asian Countries) has shown a much higher growth rate in output compared to Japan and the rest of the World in the recent period. However, because of the size of its economy, Japan is crucial for forging regional trade in Asia. In this context, it is important to see growth in Asia's trade including Japan. It is obvious that the inclusion of Japan in Asia would bring down the growth rate in Asia's trade during the decade of 1990s. The exact change can be seen by comparing information in Tables 3.3 and 3.4. Table 3.4 shows that Asia's total and agricultural and non-agricultural trade increased at a faster rate than world trade even when Japan is included with the DAC group. Similarly, intra Asia import and exports have risen at a much faster rate than extra Asia trade. Intra Asia trade in non-agricultural products followed a trend growth rate close to 9 per cent compared to 3.95 per cent growth rate in extra Asia import and 7.22 per cent growth in extra Asia exports.

Growth rates in Japan's trade were also seen by looking at its exports and imports to developing Asian countries and to rest of the World. Japan's import from Asia increased annually at the rate of 8 per cent during 1991-2000. Compared to this, its imports from the rest of the World witnessed a meagre, 1.42 per cent growth. Second, Japan's export to Asian countries followed a growth rate of 4.91 per cent compared to 2.70 per cent for exports to rest of the World. In the case of DAC, their import from Japan increased annually at the rate of 4.91 per cent which is much lower compared to the growth rate in their imports from outside Asia. DAC exports to the countries outside Asia also witnessed a higher growth compared to its exports to Japan. The difference was small in the case of non-agricultural products but it was quite large for agricultural products. Agricultural exports from DAC to Japan increased merely by 0.30 per cent per annum compared to the 4.73 per cent growth rate in the exports to countries outside Asia and 5.67 per cent growth rate to countries within DAC.

3.3 Changes in Asia's Share in World Trade

An obvious consequence of the higher growth rate in Asia's trade compared to world trade is an increase in the share of Asia in world trade. Similarly, a higher growth rate in intra regional trade compared to extra regional trade implies changes in the regional concentration of trade. These changes can be seen from the information presented in Tables 3.6 to 3.8.

Developing Asian Countries accounted for 14.1 per cent of world import and a slightly higher per cent of world export during the beginning of the decade of the 1990s. The share in import jumped to 19 per cent in the next three years while exports witnessed an increase to 18 per cent. During the next five years the share in imports dropped to 16.1 per cent but exports maintained a tempo of increase, though somewhat slowly as compared to the first half of the 1990s. The net result has been that the share of DAC in the total world trade moved up sharply in the first half of the 1990s but saw a small deterioration during the second half of the 1990s. The pattern has been similar in the case of agricultural as well as non-agricultural trade. In both types of products, the share of DAC in world trade by the end of twentieth century is found to be higher than that at the beginning of the decade of the 1990s but the gain has been higher in the case of non-agricultural products.

The share of total Asia, including Japan, which witnessed a slow growth in trade compared to the DAC group, also showed a similar pattern except that with the inclusion of Japan the increase in share turned out to be more modest.

TABLE 3.6

Share of DAC and Total Asia (DAC and Japan) in World Trade

	Share of DAC			Share of DAC and Japan		
	Import	Export	Total	Import	Export	Total
All Commodities						
TE 1992	14.1	14.7	14.4	19.5	23.6	21.5
TE 1995	19.0	18.0	18.5	25.0	27.1	26.1
TE 1998	17.1	19.0	18.0	22.1	26.7	24.4
TE 2000	16.1	19.5	17.8	20.8	27.1	23.9
Agriculture						
TE 1992	11.7	13.1	12.4	22.6	13.9	18.2
TE 1995	14.2	14.8	14.5	25.3	15.6	20.5
TE 1998	14.8	14.5	14.7	24.4	15.3	19.8
TE 2000	14.5	14.1	14.3	23.6	15.0	19.3
Non-agriculture						
TE 1992	14.4	14.9	14.7	19.0	25.1	22.0
TE 1995	19.7	18.5	19.1	25.0	28.8	26.9
TE 1998	17.4	19.6	18.5	21.8	28.3	25.0
TE 2000	16.3	20.2	18.3	20.4	28.5	24.5

Source: United Nations Trade Statistics Yearbook, various issues.

There are several reasons for a slowdown in Asia's share in world trade after showing a peak in the mid 1990s. The foremost reason being the Asian crisis. The second reason could be the emergence of RTAs in the world outside Asia in the post WTO period.

As intra Asia and extra Asia trade showed sharply different growth rates, there were changes in the regional concentration of trade which can be seen from Table 3.7. During the early 1990s, DACs met 37.3 per cent of their total import requirement from trade with other DACs. There was no increase in this share by the mid 1990s after which the share of intra Asia import in total imports of DAC increased sharply to 44.2 per cent by TE 1998 and 46 per cent by TE 2000. In the case of export, the regional concentration increased from 35.7 per cent during the early 1990s to 39.2 per cent by TE 1995. Reliance for export on outside Asia followed an increase between TE 1995 and TE 2000 though the share of extra regional export in total export of DAC followed a decline over the decade. Juxtaposing these regional concentration ratios over the share of DAC in world trade reveals that an increase in the DAC share in world trade did not affect the regional concentration of import but increased the regional concentration of exports. Conversely, a decrease in the DAC share in world trade was accompanied by a sharp increase in the regional concentration of imports and a small decline in the case of exports. In other words, it implies that the relatively faster growth of DAC trade coexists with faster growth of regional exports whereas relatively slower growth results in higher dependence within the region for imports.

Total trade (import plus export) of Developing Asian Countries showed a continuous increase in regional concentration throughout the decade of 1990s. The decade witnessed an increase in intra regional trade from 36.5 per cent during the early 1990s to more than 41 per cent by the end of the decade. Correspondingly, the share of trade with countries outside the group declined from 63.5 per cent to 58.4 per cent. The increase in concentration of trade within the DAC group is observed for both agricultural as well as non-agricultural commodities. However, non-agricultural trade showed a much faster growth in regional concentration as compared to agricultural trade. Second, agricultural trade did not show an increase in concentration in DAC between TE 1995 and TE 2000.

TABLE 3.7

Share (%) of Intra and Extra DAC Trade in Total DAC Trade

Coverage Period	Import		Export		Total Trade	
	Intra DAC	Extra DAC	Intra DAC	Extra DAC	Intra DAC	Extra DAC
All Commodities						
TE 1992	37.3	62.7	35.7	64.3	36.5	63.5
TE 1995	37.1	62.9	39.2	60.8	38.1	61.9
TE 1998	44.2	55.8	39.6	60.4	41.8	58.2
TE 2000	46.0	54.0	38.0	62.0	41.6	58.4
Agriculture						
TE 1992	39.4	60.6	35.2	64.8	37.2	62.8
TE 1995	41.1	58.9	39.5	60.5	40.3	59.7
TE 1998	40.9	59.1	41.8	58.2	41.4	58.6
TE 2000	40.1	59.9	41.1	58.9	40.6	59.4
Non-agriculture						
TE 1992	37.0	63.0	35.8	64.2	36.4	63.6
TE 1995	36.6	63.4	39.1	60.9	37.8	62.2
TE 1998	44.5	55.5	39.4	60.6	41.8	58.2
TE 2000	46.7	53.3	37.7	62.3	41.7	58.3

Source: United Nations Trade Statistics Yearbook, various issues.

As there was lot of divergence in the growth rate of trade among the DACs and between DAC and Japan it was considered imperative to examine the changes in concentration of trade between Japan and DAC. Japan supplied more than one fifth of the total merchandise import and offered a market for more than 13 per cent of the merchandise export of the DAC group during the early 1990s (Table 3.8). The share of Japan dropped by 3 percentage points in the case of imports and two percentage points in the case of exports. This decline is much bigger than the decline in the share of Japan in world trade. Share of Japan in the total trade of DAC declined from 17 per cent to 14.2 per cent during 1990s which is much higher than the decline in Japan's share in global trade. The main reason for this is that the growth rate in Japan's trade during 1990s could not keep pace with the growth rate in trade originating in other Asian countries.

Among the two groups of products Japan purchased more than one fourth of agricultural and 11.5 per cent of non-agricultural exports of all Developing Asian Countries during early 1990s (Table 3.8). By the end of the century, Japan purchased only one fifth of the total agricultural exports of DAC. The decline in share of exports of non-agricultural products to Japan was only 1.1 percentage point. However, Japan's share in DAC imports of non-agricultural products declined from 23.1 per cent to 19.3 per cent over the decade. These patterns show that during the decade of the 1990s growth in agricultural exports from DAC countries far exceeded their demand in Japan and the demand for non-agricultural imports in DAC far exceeded what Japan exported to them. Despite these reversals in

Japan-DAC trade, Japan remains a very big trading partner for DAC for agricultural exports and non-agricultural imports.

TABLE 3.8

Share of Japan in World Trade and DAC Trade

Coverage Period	Share in World Trade %			Share in DAC Trade %		
	Import	Export	Total	Import	Export	Total
All Commodities						
TE 1992	5.4	8.9	7.1	20.9	13.2	17.0
TE 1995	6.0	9.1	7.6	19.4	12.3	16.0
TE 1998	5.0	7.6	6.3	18.1	11.5	14.6
TE 2000	4.6	7.5	6.1	17.8	11.2	14.2
Agriculture						
TE 1992	10.9	0.8	5.8	4.5	25.6	15.6
TE 1995	11.1	0.8	6.0	4.1	24.0	14.3
TE 1998	9.6	0.8	5.2	3.8	20.6	12.1
TE 2000	9.1	0.8	5.0	4.0	20.1	12.0
Non-agriculture						
TE 1992	4.5	10.2	7.4	23.1	11.5	17.2
TE 1995	5.3	10.4	7.8	21.1	10.9	16.2
TE 1998	4.4	8.6	6.5	19.8	10.6	14.9
TE 2000	4.1	8.4	6.2	19.3	10.4	14.4

Source: United Nations Trade Statistics Yearbook, various issues.

Another point worth mentioning here is that Japan's trade with DAC was growing at a faster rate as compared to Japan's trade with rest of the World but DAC trade with rest of the World was growing much faster than DAC trade with Japan. This shows that for Japan the importance of Developing Asian Countries for trade purposes has increased during the 1990s whereas the importance of Japan for DAC has declined in the same period. Consequently, it turns out that the trade concentration between DAC and Japan declined during the 1990s in contrast to the considerable increase in trade concentration in DAC group. There are several reasons for that. The most important one seems to be the growth rates of output in DAC and Japan.

4

Countrywise Trade Trends

THIS chapter looks at various dimensions of trade for all the major economies in Asia. It begins by presenting the volume of inter country trade between pairs of Asian countries during the recent triennium and the growth rate in inter country trade during the last decade. It then proceeds to analyse changes in share of inter country trade in each country's total trade. The third section compares the growth rate in trade of each country with DAC and World. The changes in each country's trade share with DAC and World are discussed in Section 4.4.

4.1 Volume and Growth of Inter Country Trade

There is tremendous diversity in Asia with respect to size of the country, economic policy regime, trade liberalisation, level of economic development and socio cultural aspects. As a result of all these and other relevant factors there is tremendous variation in aspects of trade in different countries. Volume of inter country trade and each country's trade with Asia and World during the recent triennium is presented in Table 4.1 and growth rates in trade between trienniums ending 1990 and 2000 are presented in Table 4.2.

The total trade of Japan (exports plus imports) was valued at $ 752.6 billion during triennium ending 2000. Out of this, trade with Developing Asian Countries was $ 292.3 billion. Among Developing Asian Countries (DAC), China traded goods with World for $ 380 billion and with DAC for $ 135 billion. Korea comes next to China with trade volume exceeding $ 273 billion followed by Singapore having a trade volume of $ 237 billion. Out of these two countries, Singapore trades much more with Developing Asian Countries as compared to Korea. Malaysia and Thailand comes in the medium size trade power with a total trade at $ 153 and $ 112 billion respectively. In the remaining countries, the value of trade was below $ 100 billion. Trade volume for India was $ 84 billion and for Indonesia around $ 81 billion. Merchandise trade in Philippines was around $ 68 billion. Total volume of trade ranged between 11 to 25 billion $ in the case of Bangladesh, Sri Lanka, Pakistan and Vietnam.

Japan is the biggest trading partner in Asia for all Asian countries except for Bangladesh, Malaysia and Singapore. Bangladesh trades more with India while Singapore and Malaysia trade more with each other than with Japan. The biggest trading partner within the DAC group was Korea for China and Indonesia; Singapore for India, Thailand, Vietnam and Philippines; India for Sri Lanka; and China for Korea and Pakistan.

Growth rates in inter country trade shows that between TE 1990 and TE 2000, the China–Vietnam trade increased

TABLE 4.1

Inter Country Trade Among Asian Countries During TE 2000, US $ Million

	Bangladesh	China	India	Indonesia	Korea	Malaysia	Pakistan	Philippines	Singapore	Sri Lanka	Thailand	Vietnam	Japan
Bangladesh	—	686	1051	197	446	141	133	9	700	12	193	16	584
China	686	—	2309	4451	25546	5360	847	2006	9756	280	4761	1723	69457
India	**1051**	**2309**	—	**1329**	**2264**	**2589**	**270**	**193**	**3477**	**575**	**902**	**162**	**4801**
Indonesia	197	4451	1329	—	5870	2747	303	811	4345	183	2044	708	17192
Korea	446	25546	2264	5870	—	6473	603	3849	8178	447	2824	1805	39888
Malaysia	141	5360	2589	2747	6473	—	613	2706	31648	199	5216	634	23543
Pakistan	133	847	270	303	603	613	—	26	367	122	221	15	951
Philippines	9	2006	193	811	3849	2706	26	—	5065	16	1744	404	12652
Singapore	700	9756	3477	4345	8178	31648	367	5065	—	500	9260	2652	25564
Sri Lanka	12	280	575	183	447	199	122	16	500	—	208	13	742
Thailand	193	4761	902	2044	2824	5216	221	1744	9260	208	—	971	20937
Vietnam	16	1723	162	708	1805	634	15	404	2652	13	971	—	3764
Japan	584	69457	4801	17192	39888	23543	951	12652	25564	742	20937	3764	—
Asia	4262	135506	20478	30386	79686	64823	4351	21910	106781	3865	37636	13100	292303
World	11824	380087	84245	81497	273927	153793	18984	67882	237568	11292	112397	24753	752600

Note: Korea refers to Republic of Korea

Source: 1. United Nations Trade Statistics Yearbook, various issues.

2. Direction of Trade Statistics Yearbook, IMF.

at the fastest rate, 83.4 per cent per year (Table 4.2). One of the reasons for this high growth rate is that inter country trade between these two countries was very small during the base period. The second fastest increase took place between Korea and China with an annual growth of 40.5 per cent. In most of the cases, inter country trade in the DAC group was increasing annually at more than 10 per cent. There were a few cases where inter country trade showed a decline. These include trade between (i) Sri Lanka and Bangladesh; (ii) Pakistan and Philippines; and (iii) Pakistan and Japan.

Bangladesh showed the highest growth rate in its trade with India—an annual increase of 19 per cent. Bangladesh's trade with China, Indonesia, Thailand and Korea was increasing annually in the range of 10 to 15.6 per cent. There was a less than 2.5 per cent growth in its trade with Pakistan and Japan. China's trade with all Asian countries was increasing by more than 10 per cent annually except with Pakistan. India's trade also showed a growth rate of more than 10 per cent during 1990s with all Asian countries except Japan. Among various countries India's trade was growing fastest with China with an annual rate of increase placed at 28.4 per cent. Trade between India and Indonesia was increasing by more than 24 per cent annually. Like India, Indonesia also showed a double digit growth in trade with all developing Asian countries.

Korea's trade with India, Indonesia, Singapore, Philippines and Malaysia was increasing at the rate of 12 to 20 per cent. Its trade with Thailand recorded a growth rate of around 10 per cent and with Pakistan around 5 per cent. Malaysia's trade was growing fastest with Vietnam and slowest with Pakistan and Japan. Philippines trade with all

TABLE 4.2

Growth Rate in Inter Country Trade Among Asian Countries between TE 1990 and TE 2000

	Bangladesh	China	India	Indo-nesia	Korea	Malaysia	Pakistan	Phili-ppines	Singa-pore	Sri Lanka	Thailand	Viet-nam	Japan
Bangladesh	—	15.6	19.0	13.2	10.2	10.9	2.3	12.0	7.7	–6.0	11.3	9.1	2.1
China	15.6	—	28.4	15.3	40.5	17.7	6.3	20.3	13.0	10.6	14.4	83.4	14.0
India	**19.0**	**28.4**	—	**24.1**	**14.1**	**15.1**	**13.5**	**11.9**	**13.0**	**17.7**	**10.2**	**13.3**	**3.0**
Indonesia	13.2	15.3	24.1	—	12.5	16.5	12.3	13.8	11.0	18.7	19.2	33.1	0.5
Korea	10.2	40.5	14.1	12.5	—	13.1	4.8	19.8	13.3	13.9	9.8		
Malaysia	10.9	17.7	15.1	16.5	13.1	—	8.7	19.9	11.3	10.0	14.9	36.5	9.6
Pakistan	2.3	6.3	13.5	12.3	4.8	8.7	—	–6.3	4.1	1.2	4.1	23.7	-4.5
Philippines	12.0	20.3	11.9	13.8	19.8	19.9	–6.3	—	20.4	14.2	21.9	27.3	12.4
Singapore	7.7	13.0	13.0	11.0	13.3	11.3	4.1	20.4	—	9.6	9.5		6.5
Sri Lanka	–6.0	10.6	17.7	18.7	13.9	10.0	1.2	14.2	9.6	—	9.0	34.8	6.2
Thailand	11.3	14.4	10.2	19.2	9.8	14.9	4.1	21.9	9.5	9.0	—	35.1	6.8
Vietnam	9.1	83.4	13.3	33.1		36.5	23.7	27.3		34.8	35.1	—	22.4
Japan	2.1	14.0	3.0	0.5		9.6	–4.5	12.4	6.5	6.2	6.8	22.4	—
Asia	14.0	11.6	17.5	12.1	17.0	13.6	6.4	17.1	11.5	13.4	12.3	32.8	7.1
World	9.3	13.3	8.6	7.5	8.3	12.4	4.7	13.8	9.4	10.8	9.3	18.4	4.5

Note: Growth rates are point to point compound growth rate in %.

Source: Same as in Table 4.1

Asian countries was growing at more than 10 per cent rate annually except with Pakistan. Singapore's trade with China, India, Korea, Indonesia, Malaysia and Philippines was increasing at more than 10 per cent. The rate of growth was 9.5 per cent in the case of trade with Sri Lanka and Thailand, 7.7 per cent with Bangladesh, 6.5 per cent with Japan and a mere 4.1 per cent with Pakistan. Pakistan's trade during 1990s showed more than 10 per cent annual growth with India, Indonesia and Vietnam and relatively slower growth with other Asian countries. Japan's trade was growing at more than 10 per cent with only three Asian countries namely China, Philippines and Vietnam.

4.2 Share of Inter Country Trade in Total Country Trade

The magnitude and importance of inter country trade in the total trade of each country and changes therein during the last decade are presented in Table 4.3. The information is presented in the form of a matrix which can be divided in two parts. The upper half presents the share of inter country trade in the total trade of country in the 'row' and the lower half presents the share of country in the 'column'. The share reveals that during TE 1990s Japan was the biggest trading partner for all developing Asian countries. All these countries transacted about 10 per cent or more of their merchandise trade with Japan during 1988-90. The share of trade with Japan was as high as 41 per cent of the total trade of Indonesia and more than 20 per cent of the total trade of Thailand and Philippines. Trade liberalisation followed during 1990s, economic recession in the economy of Japan and other developments during the decade eroded

TABLE 4.3

Inter Country Trade among Asian Countries as Per cent of their Total Trade

Country		Bangla-desh	China	India	Indo-nesia	Korea	Malay-sia	Pakis-tan	Phili-ppines	Singa-pore	Sri Lanka	Thai-land	Viet-nam	Japan
Bangladesh	1988-1990	—	3.32	3.80	1.17	3.48	1.04	2.17	0.06	6.85	0.47	1.37	0.14	9.77
	1998-2000	—	5.80	8.89	1.66	3.77	1.19	1.12	0.07	5.92	0.10	1.63	0.14	4.94
China	1988-1990	0.15	—	0.17	0.98	0.78	0.96	0.42	0.29	2.63	0.09	1.14	0.00	17.06
	1998-2000	0.18	—	0.61	1.17	6.72	1.41	0.22	0.53	2.57	0.07	1.25	0.45	18.27
India	**1988-1990**	**0.50**	**0.52**	—	**0.42**	**1.65**	**1.73**	**0.21**	**0.17**	**2.79**	**0.31**	**0.93**	**0.13**	**9.68**
	1998-2000	**1.25**	**2.74**	—	**1.58**	**2.69**	**3.07**	**0.32**	**0.23**	**4.13**	**0.68**	**1.07**	**0.19**	**5.70**
Indonesia	1988-1990	0.14	2.71	0.39	—	4.57	1.51	0.24	0.56	3.88	0.08	0.89	0.10	41.32
	1998-2000	0.24	5.46	1.63	—	7.20	3.37	0.37	0.99	5.33	0.22	2.51	0.87	21.10
Korea	1988-1990	0.14	0.69	0.49	1.46	—	1.53	0.30	0.51	1.90	0.10	0.90	na	na
	1998-2000	0.16	9.33	0.83	2.14	—	2.36	0.22	1.40	2.99	0.16	1.03	0.66	14.56
Malaysia	1988-1990	0.10	2.19	1.33	1.25	3.95	—	0.56	0.92	22.54	0.16	2.70	0.06	19.58
	1998-2000	0.09	3.49	1.68	1.79	4.21	—	0.40	1.76	20.58	0.13	3.39	0.41	15.31
Pakistan	1988-1990	0.88	3.82	0.63	0.80	3.14	2.23	—	0.41	2.05	0.91	1.23	0.02	12.62
	1998-2000	0.70	4.46	1.42	1.60	3.17	3.23	—	0.14	1.93	0.64	1.16	0.08	5.01
Philippines	1988-1990	0.02	1.69	0.34	1.20	3.41	2.37	0.27	—	4.26	na	1.29	0.19	21.12
	1998-2000	0.01	2.95	0.28	1.19	5.67	3.99	0.04	—	7.46	na	2.57	0.60	18.64

Contd. ...

...Table 4.3 Contd. ...

		Bangla-desh	China	India	Indo-nesia	Korea	Malay-sia	Pakis-tan	Phili-ppines	Singa-pore	Sri Lanka	Thai-land	Viet-nam	Japan
Singapore	1988-1990	0.34	2.96	1.06	1.58	2.42	11.14	0.25	0.82	—	0.21	3.85	na	13.99
	1998-2000	0.29	4.11	1.46	1.83	3.44	13.32	0.15	2.13	—	0.21	3.90	1.12	10.76
Sri Lanka	1988-1990	0.56	2.53	2.79	0.81	3.01	1.89	2.68	0.10	4.95	—	2.17	0.02	10.00
	1998-2000	0.11	2.48	5.10	1.62	3.96	1.77	1.08	0.14	4.42	—	1.84	0.12	6.57
Thailand	1988-1990	0.14	2.69	0.74	0.76	2.41	2.81	0.32	0.52	8.09	0.19	—	0.10	23.43
	1998-2000	0.17	4.24	0.80	1.82	2.51	4.64	0.20	1.55	8.24	0.19	—	0.86	18.63
Vietnam	1988-1990	0.15	0.09	1.02	0.89	na	0.62	0.04	0.79	na	0.01	1.05	—	10.90
	1998-2000	0.07	6.96	0.66	2.86	7.29	2.56	0.06	1.63	10.71	0.05	3.92	—	15.20
Japan	1988-1990	0.10	3.84	0.73	3.36	na	1.93	0.31	0.81	2.79	0.08	2.23	0.10	—
	1998-2000	0.08	9.23	0.64	2.28	5.30	3.13	0.13	1.68	3.40	0.10	2.78	0.50	—

Note: Figures are share of trade between i and j as per cent of total trade of country in the row.

Source: Same as in Table 4.1

the high share and strong trade partnership with Japan for all Asian countries except China and Vietnam both of which are unique in showing an increase in the share of their trade with Japan in their total trade. The increase was modest in the case of China but quite sharp in the case of Vietnam.

Japan continues to be the biggest trading partner for Indonesia despite a steep decline in the inter country trade share in Indonesia's total trade from 41.3 per cent during TE 1990 to 21.10 per cent during TE 2000. The decline was relatively small in the case of Thailand, Malaysia, Singapore and Philippines. Inter country trade share with Japan reduced to about half in the case of South Asian countries.

It is interesting to point out that share of Japan's trade with Asian countries in Japan's total trade did not show much symmetry with the inter country trade of Asian countries with Japan. The main reason for this is the difference in rates of growth of trade of Japan and other Asian countries. For instance, share of inter country trade with Japan show decline in total trade of Malaysia, Thailand, Singapore and Philippines but it shows increase in total trade of Japan. Similarly, the Japan–China trade shows a two and half times increase in terms of share in Japan's total trade but a very small (only 7 per cent) increase in terms of share in China's total trade.

During the 1990s, Bangladesh expanded its trade with India more rapidly than with other Asian countries. As a result India came to occupy the status of biggest trading partner for Bangladesh accounting for about 9 per cent of Bangladesh's total trade, the position enjoyed by Japan a decade ago. Singapore and China were other important trading partners for Bangladesh and the trade with China was expanding very fast. There was increase in share of its inter country trade with Malaysia, Thailand and Philippines.

There was a small to big increase in the proportion of China's trade with Asian countries except with Pakistan. Korea was its biggest trading partner after Japan in Asia. The proportion of India's trade with all Developing Asian Countries showed an increase during 1990s. Similarly, Indonesia was also trading proportionately more with DAC compared to a decade earlier. The share of Indo-China trade in India's total trade increased from 0.52 per cent during TE 1990 to 2.74 per cent during TE 2000. Large increases were also observed in India's trade with Malaysia, Indonesia, Korea, Singapore and Bangladesh. Korea's trade with China increased from below 1 per cent of its total trade a decade ago to 9.33 per cent in the recent years. The proportion of its trade with all developing Asian countries showed an increase except with Pakistan. Malaysia was also trading proportionately more with the DAC group now than 10 years before, except with Pakistan, Singapore and Sri Lanka. However, Singapore remained the biggest trading partner of Malaysia in Asia accounting for more than one fifth of its trade.

Pakistan was trading proportionately less with the Philippines, Bangladesh, Singapore, Thailand and Vietnam and more with China, India, Indonesia, Malaysia and Korea. China was close to becoming its biggest trading partner in Asia with more than a four per cent share. The inter country trade share of the Philippines shows an increase with China, Korea, Malaysia, Singapore and Thailand and decline with other Asian countries. After Japan, its trade was highest with Singapore. Trade between Singapore and Malaysia increased from 11.14 per cent of the total Singapore trade during TE 1990 to 13.32 per cent during TE 2000 making Malaysia its largest trading partner substituting Japan. Singapore was also trading proportionately much more with China, Korea and Philippines recently compared to 10 years before. Sri Lanka's trade with India increased from 2.79 per cent of its total trade during TE 1990 to 5.10 per cent during TE 2000. Similarly, trade with Indonesia and Korea increased from 0.81 and 3.01 per cent to 1.62 and 3.96 per cent, respectively. Sri Lanka trades relatively less with China, Pakistan, Bangladesh, Malaysia, Singapore and Thailand. Thailand was trading proportionately more with all developing Asian countries except Pakistan. Vietnam was expanding its trade very fast with all East Asian countries.

4.3 Growth Rate in Countrywise Trade with DAC and Rest of the World

The combined picture of growth rates in inter country trade among Asian countries is presented and compared with the growth in their trade with the rest of the World in respect of each country in Table 4.4. Growth rates have also been presented separately for import and export. The trade of each Asian country with the group of DAC increased at a much faster rate than trade with rest of the World (ROW) during 1991-2000. China and Cambodia were two exceptions. China's trade with ROW increased annually at 15.47 per cent compared to a 9.33 per cent rate of increase in its trade with DAC. The difference was minor in the case of import but very large in the case of export. China's export to ROW increased at the rate of 19.1 per cent compared to the 8.10 per cent growth rate in its export to DAC. The growth rate in imports was 11.79 per cent from ROW and 10.93 per cent from DAC. In the case of Cambodia, the trade with ROW showed a growth rate of 29 per cent and with DAC, 24 per cent.

Japan's trade with countries outside Asia increased annually by 2.90 per cent. Its trade with Asian countries increased by more than double the growth rate with ROW. The growth rate was higher for both, imports as well as exports.

TABLE 4.4

Growth Rate in Export, Import and Total Trade in Asian Countries, 1991-2000

(per cent/annum)

Country	DAC			Rest of the World		
	Export	Import	Total Trade	Export	Import	Total Trade
Bangladesh	4.21	16.06	14.91	11.67	6.69	9.00
Cambodia	19.81	25.49	24.24	44.54	15.51	29.06
China mainland	8.10	10.93	9.33	19.10	11.79	15.47
China Hongkong	7.85	8.62	8.31	6.16	5.00	5.70
India	**14.56**	**25.95**	**19.96**	**8.60**	**8.62**	**8.61**
Indonesia	11.11	5.75	9.04	5.48	–0.68	2.93
Korea	14.40	11.13	13.16	8.15	5.47	6.76
Malaysia	11.05	10.86	10.96	11.53	6.39	8.93
Myanmar	8.25	15.37	13.30			
Nepal	28.68	20.61	21.42	5.73	–3.65	0.29
Pakistan	2.20	5.24	3.86	4.01	1.70	2.73
Philippines	27.93	14.61	19.70	17.26	10.52	13.69
Singapore	10.97	9.09	10.11	7.67	5.83	6.65
Sri Lanka	10.08	9.95	9.95	10.93	7.80	9.60
Thailand	14.33	5.26	9.46	7.37	3.11	5.19
Vietnam	24.14	26.94	25.84	23.52	17.29	20.78
Japan	4.86	7.65	6.01	2.71	3.13	2.90

Source: Same as in Table 4.1.

Bangladesh's trade increased by 9 per cent annually with the rest of the World and by close to 15 per cent with Developing Asian Countries. However, the picture was different for exports and imports. Its exports to ROW showed much higher growth than to DAC whereas the reverse was true for imports. A similar situation holds for Pakistan and to some extent for Sri Lanka–with exports showing a faster growth to ROW than to DAC but imports from DAC showing higher growth rates as compared to imports from ROW. In the case of China both imports and exports to ROW were increasing at a faster rate than to DAC whereas the reverse was true for most of the other DACs. Nepal and Indonesia show a decline in imports from rest of the World.

Countrywise growth rates in trade with DAC *vis à vis* ROW were 19.96 and 8.61 for India, 9.04 and 2.93 for Indonesia, 13.16 and 6.76 for Korea, 10.96 and 8.93 for Malaysia, 21.42 and 0.29 per cent for Nepal, 3.86 and 2.73 per cent for Pakistan, 19.70 and 13.69 for Philippines, 10.11 and 6.65 for Singapore, 9.46 and 5.19 for Thailand and 25.84 and 20.78 for Vietnam. This shows that most of the Asian countries have moved towards an Asia centric trade during the last decade. In the case of China and Cambodia, dependence on Asia for trade was becoming less compared to that with ROW.

4.4 Countrywise Distribution of Trade over DAC and ROW

Different rates of growth in trade with DAC and ROW have changed the share of these two groups in the total trade of each country. The shares as obtained during the three years ending 1990 and 2000 are presented in Table 4.5.

There is a substantial increase in share of trade with DAC in total trade of all Asian countries except China and Cambodia. In the case of China, trade with Asia constituted 41 per cent of its total trade during TE 1990 which declined to 35.6 per cent in next ten years. A similar decline is noticeable in the case of Cambodia but still it trades more than half of total trade volume with DAC.

TABLE 4.5

Distribution of Trade by Various Countries over DAC and Rest of the World

(per cent)

Country	Time Period	DAC			Rest of the World		
		Export	Import	Total Trade	Export	Import	Total Trade
Bangladesh	1988-1990	11.6	28.8	23.7	88.4	71.2	76.3
	1998-2000	6.5	52.0	36.0	93.5	48.0	64.0
Cambodia	1988-1990	83.3	55.4	67.3	16.7	44.6	32.7
	1998-2000	31.7	77.1	56.7	68.3	22.9	43.3
China mainland	1988-1990	51.3	31.8	41.4	48.7	68.2	58.6
	1998-2000	33.6	38.2	35.7	66.4	61.8	64.3
China Hongkong	1988-1990	41.1	57.6	49.3	58.9	42.4	50.7
	1998-2000	45.9	66.4	56.4	54.1	33.6	43.6
India	**1988-1990**	**13.2**	**10.8**	**11.8**	**86.8**	**89.2**	**88.2**
	1998-2000	**22.9**	**25.4**	**24.3**	**77.1**	**74.6**	**75.7**
Indonesia	1988-1990	24.2	24.6	24.4	75.8	75.4	75.6
	1998-2000	38.0	35.9	37.3	62.0	64.1	62.7
Korea	1988-1990	15.8	10.9	13.4	84.2	89.1	86.6
	1998-2000	34.7	22.4	29.1	65.3	77.6	70.9
Malaysia	1988-1990	42.5	32.4	37.7	57.5	67.6	62.3
	1998-2000	43.0	41.1	42.1	57.0	58.9	57.9
Myanmar	1988-1990	60.8	57.1	58.9	39.2	42.9	41.1
	1998-2000	56.5	91.7	79.7	43.5	8.3	20.3
Nepal	1988-1990	21.5	37.3	33.8	78.5	62.7	66.2
	1998-2000	28.8	71.1	58.1	71.2	28.9	41.9

Contd. ...

...Table 4.5 Contd. ...

Country	Time Period	DAC Export	DAC Import	DAC Total Trade	Rest of the World Export	Rest of the World Import	Rest of the World Total Trade
Pakistan	1988-1990	21.5	18.2	19.5	78.5	81.8	80.5
	1998-2000	20.3	25.1	22.9	79.7	74.9	77.1
Philippines	1988-1990	18.2	28.4	24.3	81.8	71.6	75.7
	1998-2000	30.4	34.3	32.3	69.6	65.7	67.7
Singapore	1988-1990	42.2	32.4	37.0	57.8	67.6	63.0
	1998-2000	49.7	40.0	44.9	50.3	60.0	55.1
Sri Lanka	1988-1990	11.3	38.1	27.1	88.7	61.9	72.9
	1998-2000	8.4	54.4	34.2	91.6	45.6	65.8
Thailand	1988-1990	23.8	27.0	25.6	76.2	73.0	74.4
	1998-2000	34.3	32.6	33.5	65.7	67.4	66.5
Vietnam	1988-1990	20.1	14.7	16.8	79.9	85.3	83.2
	1998-2000	39.4	65.2	52.9	60.6	34.8	47.1
Japan	1988-1990	30.3	30.3	30.3	69.7	69.7	69.7
	1998-2000	38.0	39.9	38.8	62.0	60.1	61.2

Source: Same as in Table 4.1.

Countries like Hongkong, Myanmar, Nepal, and Vietnam have not only increased the proportion of their trade with DAC but they also trade more than half of their total trade volume with DAC.

Bangladesh traded three fourths of its goods with ROW during TE 1990 but this has come down to less than two third during TE 2000. However, this country exported very little (11.6 per cent) to developing countries of Asia region which was further reduced to 6.5 per cent. The situation of Sri Lanka is almost similar. These two countries have increased their dependence upon DAC to meet more than half of their requirement for imported goods but find a very narrow and shrinking market for the sale of their produce in DAC markets.

Ten years back, Japan shared 70 per cent of its trade with ROW and 30 per cent with Asian developing countries. In recent years, the share of its trade with DAC has increased to 39 per cent. The decline in share of trade with ROW has been very high in the case of Vietnam, Nepal and Myanmar.

Among all the Asian countries India transacted a minimum proportion (11.8%) of its merchandise trade with Developing Asian Countries during TE 1990. In next ten years it shared more than 24 per cent of its trade with DAC, which left Pakistan as the least trading country with DAC.

Trade shares were also studied with Japan and with ROW excluding Japan. In some cases a decline in the share of Asian countries' trade with ROW including Japan (presented in Table 4.5) was due to a decline in the share of trade with Japan. Table 4.6 isolates trade share with Japan from ROW. This shows that when Japan is excluded, there was no decline in trade share with ROW for Hongkong, Indonesia, Malaysia and Pakistan. Obviously, there is a steep decline in their trade shared with Japan. There was a decline in trade shared with Japan during the 1990s and also in trade shared with ROW for the remaining Asian countries except China and Vietnam. China showed an increase in trade shared with Japan and with countries outside Asia. Vietnam showed an increase in trade shared with Japan but a substantial decline in trade shared with non Asian countries.

TABLE 4.6

Changes in Share of Countrywise Trade with Developing Asia, Japan and Rest of the World

(per cent)

Country	Period	Developing Asia	Japan	Rest of the World	Country Share in World Trade
Bangladesh	1988-1990	23.7	11.1	65.2	0.08
	1998-2000	36.0	5.8	58.1	0.10
China mainland	1988-1990	41.4	16.7	41.9	1.80
	1998-2000	35.7	18.2	46.2	3.23
China Hongkong	1988-1990	49.3	23.2	27.5	2.39
	1998-2000	56.4	15.7	27.5	3.19
India	**1988-1990**	**11.8**	**9.5**	**79.4**	**0.60**
	1998-2000	**24.3**	**5.7**	**70.0**	**0.72**
Indonesia	1988-1990	24.4	34.5	41.1	0.65
	1998-2000	37.3	19.0	43.7	0.69
Korea	1988-1990	13.4	24.1	62.5	2.03
	1998-2000	29.1	14.8	56.1	2.33
Malaysia	1988-1990	37.7	19.7	42.5	0.79
	1998-2000	42.1	15.8	42.1	1.31
Pakistan	1988-1990	19.5	11.8	68.7	0.20
	1998-2000	22.9	5.2	71.8	0.16
Philippines	1988-1990	24.3	19.2	56.6	0.31
	1998-2000	32.3	16.1	51.7	0.58
Singapore	1988-1990	37.0	15.2	47.7	1.59
	1998-2000	44.9	11.9	43.1	2.02
Sri Lanka	1988-1990	27.1	9.6	63.3	0.07
	1998-2000	34.2	6.9	58.8	0.10
Thailand	1988-1990	25.6	24.0	50.3	0.76
	1998-2000	33.5	18.9	47.6	0.95
Vietnam	1988-1990	16.8	9.3	73.9	0.07
	1998-2000	52.9	15.2	31.9	0.21
Japan	1988-1990	30.3	—	69.7	7.98
	1998-2000	38.8	—	61.2	6.39
Dev. Asia	1988-1990	32.4	18.1	49.5	12.96
	1998-2000	46.0	14.2	39.8	17.78

Source: Same as in Table 4.1.

The highest decline in trade share of outside Asia region was observed in the case of Vietnam with its share falling from 74 per cent during TE 1990 to 32 per cent during TE 2000. The highest decline in share of trade with Japan was observed in the case of Indonesia. Indonesia traded more than one third of its total merchandise trade with Japan at the beginning of 1990s which was more than its trade with the rest of Asia. By the end of 1990s Indonesia's share of trade with Japan plummeted to 19 per cent. Vietnam was the least trading country with Japan during TE 1990s. Alongwith Vietnam, India, Bangladesh, Pakistan and Sri Lanka shared less than 12 per cent of their trade with Japan. After that, Vietnam increased the proportion of its trade with Japan but South Asian countries remained least trading partners with Japan in Asia.

Table 4.6 also contains information on the share of each country in world trade during TE 1990 and 2000. Among all the Asian economies, Japan remained the biggest trading power though its share in world trade dropped from close to 8 per cent to 6.4 per cent. Hongkong was the second biggest trading power in Asia during TE 1990. During the decade of 1990s China improved its share in world trade significantly and emerged as the second biggest trading country after Japan with a share of 3.23 per cent. It is interesting to observe that all developing Asian countries except Pakistan improved their share in world trade during 1990s. This shows that all the developing Asian countries, barring Pakistan, performed better in trade compared to rest of the World.

5

Implications of Emerging Trade Trends in Asia

IT was demonstrated in ch. 3 that Developing Asian Countries recorded a higher growth rate in their trade compared to rest of the World during the 1990s, and a much higher growth in intra regional trade as compared to extra regional trade. These patterns in trade growth provide a useful guide for the prospects of further growth in trade through regional trading arrangements. One explanation for the disproportionate growth in regional trade is that policy regimes followed by neighbouring countries at similar stages of development also tend towards similarity. To the extent that neighbourhood characteristics encourage trade, liberalisation should encourage growth in the share of neighbourhood trade in total trade. Since liberalisation occurs in stages, trade patterns display a dynamic where growth in intra regional trade exceeds the growth in inter regional trade (Diao, Roe and Somwaru 1999). These scholars argued that if this pattern occurs, then regional trade arrangements may be entered into to further remove obstacles to trade and to avert policy reversals. We examine in this chapter whether this kind of evolution is taking place in Asia to forge regional trade arrangements.

The second rather more important aspect relating to Regional Trade Agreement (RTA) is its impact on the welfare of members of RTA and non member countries. Krugman (1995) shows that, in principle, Free Trade Areas are welfare enhancing. The impact of Regional Trade Agreements (RTA) on welfare is generally seen by examining trade creation and trade diversion within the region and outside the region. Trade creation occurs when some domestic production in a nation is replaced by lower cost import from another member nation. This is reflected in the growth of intra regional trade. This increases the welfare of the member nations as it leads to greater specialisation in production based on comparative advantage. On the other hand, trade diversion occurs when lower cost imports from outside the region (having RTA) are replaced by higher cost import from a nation within the RTA because of preferential treatment to members of the RTA. Trade diversion by itself reduces welfare because it shifts resources away from comparative advantage. This can cause a positive or negative impact on the welfare of the members but it reduces the welfare of non members (Salvitore 1990, ch.10). An attempt has been made in this chapter to examine the potential welfare effect of changes taking place in regional trade in Asia. Towards the end, the chapter discuss the strategy to take advantage of changes in regional trade pattern.

5.1 Growth Path of DAC and World Trade

Several countries in Asia started some sort of trade liberalisation in early 1990s. Implementation of Uruguay

Round Agreement (URA) led to further liberalisation of trade policies and reforms in domestic policies. This is reflected in the dismantling of trade barriers and reduction in tariff rates on imports by almost all the countries (Table 5.1). The table shows changes (reduction) in weighted tariff rates applied on imports by various countries during the period under study. All the countries in the DAC group for which information on tariff was available lowered tariffs on imports. Bangladesh had the highest tariff, around 106 per cent, during 1990; the average tariff have been brought down to 21.6 per cent in the year 2001. Similarly, India on an average levied 56.2 per cent trade weighted tariff during 1990 which have been brought down to half in the next 10 years. Pakistan brought down its tariff from 46 per cent in 1995 to 14.7 per cent during 2000. Likewise, Thailand and Philippines lowered the applied tariff from 33 and 22 per cent levels to 9.7 and 4 per cent during the decade. Similar kind of reductions have been affected by other DACs. The tariff rates during 1988-1989 were a mere 3.6 and 0.5 per cent in the case of Japan and Singapore. By the year 2001 Japan reduced the weighted tariff rate to 2.1 per cent and Singapore is reported to have made its imports totally free from tariff. This liberalisation of tariff and removal of trade restrictions is a significant factor for high growth in total DAC trade and still higher growth rate in intra regional trade.

These changes have been followed by a faster growth in intra Asia trade and share of Asia in world trade. More detailed information on these changes was obtained by looking at the yearly data during the decade of 1990s presented in Tables 5.2 to 5.4 and in Fig. 5.1 to 5.5.

TABLE 5.1

Changes in Weighted Mean of Applied Tariff on Imports in Selected Asian Countries During 1990s

Country	Beginning of 1980s	End of 1990s
Bangladesh	88.2 (1989)	21.0 (2001)
China Taiwan	32.5 (1992)	14.3 (2001)
India	**56.2 (1990)**	**28.2 (2001)**
Indonesia	13.2 (1989)	5.4 (2000)
Korea Rp.	13.6 (1988)	7.9 (1999)
Malaysia	9.9 (1988)	5.8 (1997)
Pakistan	17.5 (1995)	16.8 (2000)
Philippines	22.4 (1988)	4.0 (2001)
Singapore	0.5 (1989)	0.0 (2001)
Sri Lanka	26.9 (1990)	7.2 (2001)
Thailand	33.0 (1989)	9.7 (2000)
Vietnam	18.4 (1994)	15.1 (2001)
Japan	3.6 (1990)	2.1 (2001)

Note: Figures in parenthesis refer to the year for which tariff is reported.
Source: World Development Indicators 2003, World Bank, Washington.

Intra Asia trade accounted for 4.4 per cent of total world trade during the year 1990 after which it kept rising steadily till 1997 (Table 5.2 and Fig. 5.1). There was a small setback to the share of intra DAC trade in world trade with the beginning of Asian financial crisis during 1998 but the share recovered back to 8 per cent during the year 2000. This way, the share of trade among developing Asian countries in the world trade almost doubled between 1990 and 2000.

There was also a substantial increase in the share of extra Asia trade in world trade during the early years of the decade of 1990s. The share was extraordinarily high during 1994 which is a sort of abnormal situation. The share remained around 10.8 per cent since 1995. This shows that share of intra Asia trade did not increase at the cost of extra Asia trade.

The share of intra Asia trade in agricultural products in the world trade increased during the first half of 1990s after which it showed a small decline whereas extra Asia agricultural trade showed a small increase during the same period. These results show that trade in non-agricultural products followed an increased regional concentration but there was no evidence of such concentration in the case of agricultural trade after 1994 (Fig. 5.1 and 5.2).

Another way to examine the changes in the regional concentration in trade and to see its effect on the region's trade with the outside region is by comparing the annual rate of growth in intra and extra regional trade with a growth in world trade. These growth rates for total merchandise trade are presented in Table 5.3 and for agricultural trade in Table 5.4.

Total merchandise imports of the DAC group showed a higher growth rate than world trade in 7 out of 10 years during 1991 to 2000. Intra Asia imports increased faster than world imports in all the years except year 1998. Intra regional imports showed a higher growth than extra regional imports in seventy per cent of the cases. These patterns raise an important issue that intra regional imports can grow faster than world imports if countries in the group divert trade from other countries to the countries in the group which would imply trade diversion and hence a decline in the welfare of members outside the group. This can be seen by looking at the growth rate of total regional imports *vis à vis* the growth rate in world trade.

TABLE 5.2

Share of Intra and Extra DAC Trade in World Trade

Year	All Products			Agricultural Products		
	Intra	Extra	Total	Intra	Extra	Total
1990	4.4	8.5	12.9	4.2	7.4	11.6
1991	5.3	9.2	14.5	4.7	7.8	12.5
1992	6.0	9.6	15.6	4.9	8.2	13.1
1993	6.5	10.8	17.3	5.1	8.4	13.5
1994	7.2	12.9	20.1	6.0	8.6	14.7
1995	7.3	10.8	18.0	6.2	8.9	15.2
1996	7.7	10.8	18.5	6.2	9.0	15.3
1997	8.0	10.8	18.8	6.2	8.7	15.0
1998	7.0	9.9	16.8	5.7	8.0	13.7
1999	7.2	10.4	17.6	5.8	8.3	14.1
2000	8.0	10.9	18.9	6.0	9.3	15.3

Source: United Nations Trade Statistics Yearbook, various issues.

TABLE 5.3

Annual Growth Rate in World Trade and DAC Trade During 1990 to 2000

Year	World Trade	DAC Imports			DAC Exports		
		Total	Extra	Intra	Total	Extra	Intra
1991	0.6	13.4	8.2	23.2	14.2	9.7	23.2
1992	7.9	17.0	15.0	20.2	14.4	11.2	20.2
1993	–0.6	11.0	12.3	8.9	9.9	10.6	8.9
1994	14.4	45.7	57.5	26.5	19.9	16.0	26.5
1995	23.7	2.4	–8.7	24.8	21.3	19.0	24.8
1996	–0.2	–0.1	–3.7	5.2	4.7	4.4	5.2
1997	3.8	3.7	0.7	7.7	6.7	6.0	7.7
1998	–1.5	–18.1	–21.4	–14.0	–5.4	0.6	–14.0
1999	3.5	10.5	13.2	7.3	6.2	5.6	7.3
2000	11.9	19.7	15.9	24.3	20.3	17.9	24.3

Source: United Nations Trade Statistics Yearbook, various issues.

TABLE 5.4

Annual Rate of Growth in World Trade and DAC Trade in Agricultural Products During 1990 to 2000

Year	World Trade	DAC Imports			DAC Exports		
		Total	Extra	Intra	Total	Extra	Intra
1991	0.1	7.6	7.5	12.8	8.3	5.9	12.8
1992	6.7	14.8	14.8	11.7	9.6	8.4	11.7
1993	–3.2	–0.1	–0.1	0.7	0.6	0.5	0.7
1994	14.8	25.5	25.5	35.2	23.0	16.1	35.2
1995	17.2	27.2	27.2	21.2	15.6	11.9	21.2
1996	1.1	2.1	2.1	1.1	1.8	2.3	1.1
1997	–0.8	–1.7	–1.7	–0.8	–3.9	–6.0	–0.8
1998	–5.4	–16.4	–16.4	–13.5	–11.1	–9.3	–13.5
1999	–3.9	0.6	0.6	–3.0	–2.7	–2.5	–3.0
2000	1.5	12.6	12.6	5.8	7.7	9.0	5.8

Source: United Nations Trade Statistics Yearbook, various issues.

FIGURE 5.1

Share of DAC in World Trade: All Products

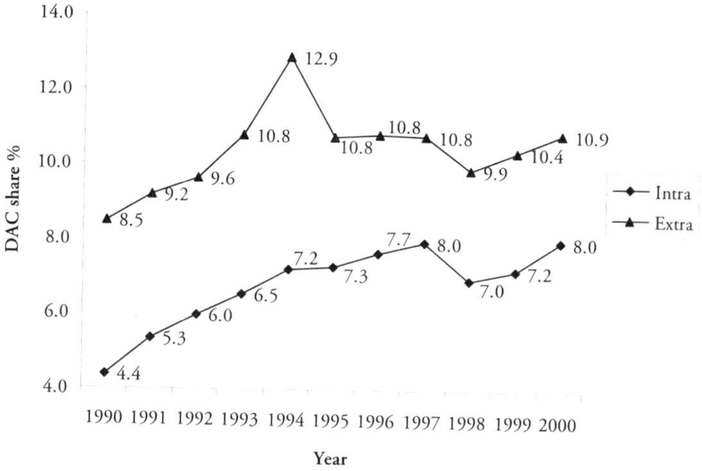

FIGURE 5.2

Share of DAC in World Trade: Agril. Products

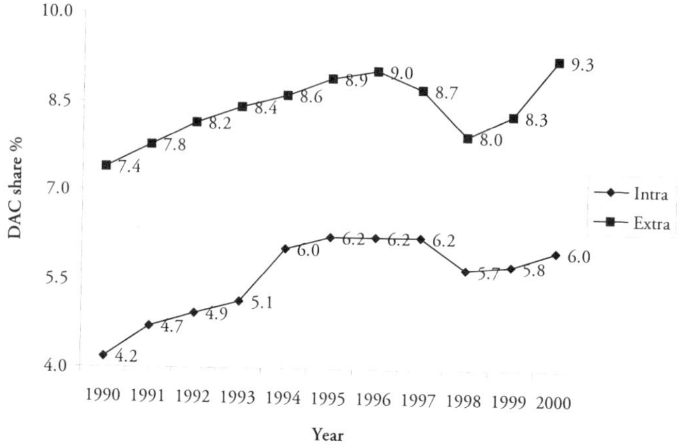

FIGURE 5.3

Share of Intra and Extra DAC Import and Export in Total DAC Trade

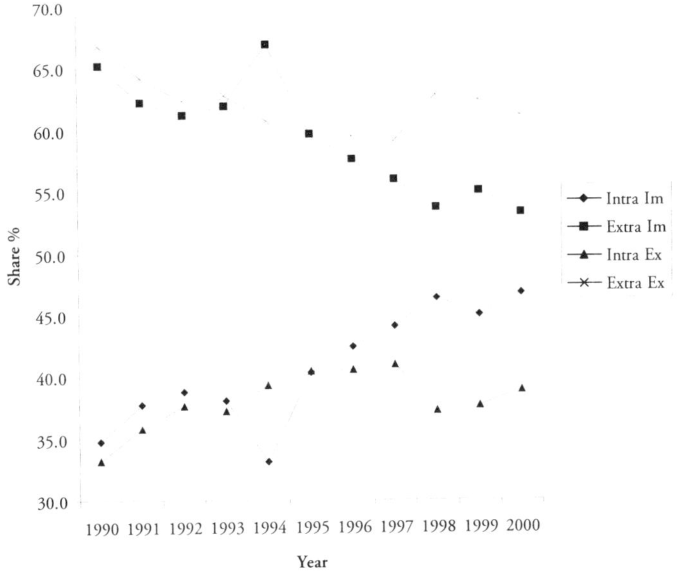

FIGURE 5.4

Growth Path of World and DAC Imports

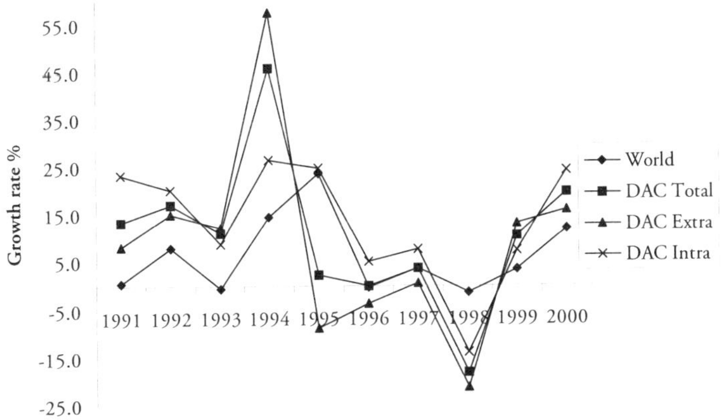

FIGURE 5.5

Growth Path of World and DAC Exports

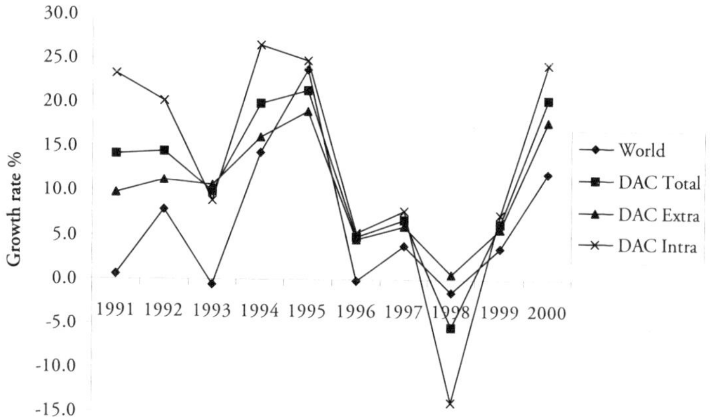

It can be observed from Table 5.2 that regional imports grew at a faster rate in seven out of ten years. Even extra regional imports grew at a faster rate than world trade in majority of the cases. Also, it has been shown in Table 5.2 that there is no decline in extra DAC trade in world trade. All these indicators show that a high growth and regional concentration in total merchandise trade among Developing Asian Countries has resulted in trade creation within the group and also outside the group.

Regional concentration and growth in Asia's export is even stronger than that observed in the case of imports. Both intra as well as extra export showed a higher growth rate than world trade in 90 per cent of the cases. Further, growth rates in intra DAC exports were higher than extra DAC in eight out of ten cases.

The growth paths of intra, extra and total DAC and world trade in agricultural products are presented in Table

5.4. Growth rates in intra and extra regional exports were higher than the growth rate in world trade in eight out of ten years. However, the growth path did not show any regional concentration in agricultural trade as incidence of intra trade having a higher growth rate than extra trade was exactly equal to the cases where extra trade showed a higher growth rate than intra trade.

The above results show that trade concentration in the group of Developing Asian Countries has increased during the decade of 1990s. The increase is attributable to non-agricultural trade, as agricultural trade did not show any increase in regional concentration.

There are several factors which affect increased regionalisation of DAC trade. The most important among these is trade liberalisation as has been shown in Table 5.1.

5.2 Trade Intensity and Trade Propensity Indices

As it has been discussed in ch.2, the share of intra regional trade in a region's total trade is considered as a very inadequate indicator of a regional bias induced by the preferential policy of members in the region. To establish a regional bias in trade one needs to prove whether countries in a region or group are trading proportionately more among themselves relative to the outside world, which is revealed accurately by the Intensity Index for intra and inter regional trade. The intensity Index, for instance, for country *a's* export to country *b* is the ratio of share of country *a's* exports going to country *b* relative to *b's* share in world import net of *a's* imports. Thus, the intensity index compares *b's* proportionate trade with country *a* compared to its trade with rest of the World. In case country *b* buys (imports) "p" per cent of total export of *a* and has the same share in import of rest of the World then its trade has no bias. If *b* buys a higher per cent of *a's* exports compared to its share in import of rest of the World than *b's* trade is biased towards *a*. As mentioned in chapter 2, if there is no regional concentration of trade then the intensity index is one. The value of the index more than 1 for intra regional trade is evidence of a regional bias in trade and intensity index of less than 1 for extra regional trade is evidence of bias against the outside region.

Changes in Index of Intensity to Trade (IIT) for the group of Developing Asian Countries and for individual countries' trade with DAC during the 1990s are presented in Table 5.5. The table shows that intra regional IIT during the early 1990s was around 2.5 whereas IIT for extra regional trade was below 1. This shows that developing Asian countries traded proportionately more among themselves than they should be trading if there was no regional bias. Similarly, these countries have been trading proportionately less with outside countries than what they should be trading if there was no regional trade bias.

Further, in order to see whether the regional concentration of trade in the DAC group was due to high concentration among a few countries or it holds true for all, IIT was computed for all major countries in Asia in respect of their trade with DAC. During TE 1990, all Asian countries except India traded disproportionately high with other Developing Asian countries and disproportionately low with the rest of the World. During TE 1990, India's trade with DAC and rest of the World was almost proportionate as IIT was close to 1 for both the cases. In the next ten years, India also started trading more with the DAC group than with the rest of the World.

TABLE 5.5

Intensity Index of Intra and Extra Regional (DAC) Trade for Major Asian Countries

Country	Intra Regional Trade Intensity		Extra Regional Trade Intensity	
	TE 1990	TE 2000	TE 1990	TE 2000
Bangladesh	1.54	1.53	0.92	0.83
China	3.70	2.39	0.66	0.72
India	**0.97**	**1.41**	**1.01**	**0.88**
Indonesia	1.97	2.17	0.86	0.73
Korea	1.21	1.86	0.98	0.81
Malaysia	3.07	2.55	0.71	0.67
Pakistan	1.56	1.29	0.92	0.90
Philippines	1.82	1.88	0.88	0.79
Singapore	3.26	2.86	0.71	0.63
Sri Lanka	1.87	1.65	0.86	0.81
Thailand	2.06	1.99	0.85	0.77
Vietnam	1.36	2.92	0.95	0.56
All DAC: Total trade	2.52[1]	2.34	0.74[1]	0.70
All DAC: Agricultural trade	3.00[1]	2.72	0.71[1]	0.70
Japan	2.16	2.07	0.77	0.67

Note: [1] Refers to TE 1992.

Source: 1. United Nations Trade Statistics Yearbook, various issues.
2. Direction of Trade Statistics Yearbook, IMF.

A strong neighbourhood bias was also found in the case of agricultural trade in DAC countries (Table 5.5) but it did not show any evidence of faster growth in intra DAC trade in most of the years during the 1990s. Nor there was any increase in share of intra regional agricultural trade after 1994. These results show that increased regionalisation of DAC trade resulted from increased regionalisation of trade in non-agricultural products. The reason for agricultural trade not showing an increased regional concentration seems to be that even during the post WTO period DAC countries did not strongly follow liberalisation of agricultural trade which remained much lesser than liberalisation of non-agricultural trade.

Figures for IIT establish that all the Asian countries have a bias towards neighbourhood trade. The policies followed by the DAC group during the 1990s have further increased a regional bias as can be seen from the increase in share of intra regional trade in the total DAC trade which witnessed an increase from 36.5 per cent to 41.6 per cent during the decade (Table 5.6). There has also been a moderately large increase in the DAC share in world trade. Because of this increase in DAC share in world trade there is small decrease in IIT but the index for intra regional and extra regional trade remains quite far from 1 showing that a strong regional bias in DAC trade continued during the decade of 1990s.

Further, a decline in extra regional IIT over time does not reveal correctly whether the increase in regionalisation of trade is causing a trade diversion for outside world. The correct measure to find out whether change in policy that increased regionalisation of trade caused an adverse affect on the region's trade with the outside world is given by the Index of Propensity to Trade (IPT). This index is obtained by multiplying IIT by openness to trade (ratio of GDP traded). An increase in propensity to trade indicates trade creation and decrease in propensity to trade indicate trade diversion. Thus, even if intensity to trade with the outside region falls, due to a change in policy that increases the regional concentration of trade, it may not result in a decline in propensity to trade if the trade to GDP ratio increases large enough.

TABLE 5.6

Index of Intensity and Propensity to Trade Intra Regionally and Extra Regionally During 1990s

Particular	TE 1992	TE 2000
1. Intra regional trade share DAC %	36.5	41.6
2. DAC share of world trade %	14.4	17.8
3. Intensity index of intra regional trade		
Imports	2.524	2.343
Exports	2.525	2.347
Total Trade	2.523	2.347
4. Intensity index of extra regional trade		
Imports	0.731	0.665
Exports	0.744	0.734
Total Trade	0.737	0.700
5. Share of GDP traded %	47.3	58.4
6. Index of propensity to trade intra regionally		
Imports	1.195	1.367
Exports	1.195	1.370
Total Trade	1.194	1.369
7. Index of Propensity to trade extra regionally		
Imports	0.346	0.388
Exports	0.352	0.428
Total Trade	0.349	0.409

Alongwith an increased regionalisation of trade, the policies followed by DAC during the decade of 1990s involved trade liberalisation which led to an increase in the proportion of GDP traded. The share of trade in GDP increased from 47.3 per cent during TE 1992 to 58.4 per cent during TE 2000. This increase in the share of trade in GDP of DAC was stronger than the decline in the Intensity Index of extra regional trade. Thus, the propensity to trade extra regionally increased from 0.349 to 0.409 during 1990 to 2000. This shows that the regional concentration (bias) in trade and increased regionalisation of DAC trade during the 1990s have been accompanied by a tendency to trade more with the rest of the World.

5.3 Implications of Growing Regionalisation of DAC trade for Outside World

The trade intensity index shows that trade among DAC has a strong neighbourhood bias. This bias has been further strengthened by the faster growth of intra regional trade compared to extra regional trade during the decade of the 1990s. Moreover, intra regional trade and the total trade of DAC show a significantly higher growth compared to world trade. This has pushed the DAC share in world trade. In the same period trade to GDP ratio of the DAC group increased by about a quarter from 47 per cent to 58 per cent. Consequently, the propensity to trade has grown extra regionally as also intra regionally. Fast growth in internal trade in the region has been accompanied by the tendency to trade more and more with the outside world. This has created trade opportunities outside DAC, i.e. external trade creation. For the world as a whole trade creation has been stronger than trade diversion because of the increased regionalisation of DAC trade during the period 1990 to 2000. In other words, this can be taken to mean that regionalisation of trade in developing Asia during the 1990s has improved welfare for developing Asia and for the rest of the World.

5.4 Implications for Trade Policy and Government Initiatives

There is clear and strong evidence that policy changes initiated by Asian countries during the last decade have led to increased regionalisation of trade in Developing Asian Countries. Further, this increased regionalisation has been accompanied by trade creation and not trade diversion. What are the implications of this kind of emerging trends to enhance the benefit to countries in the region? Can governments take some action to help the countries harness an advantage out of this situation? If yes, how it can be done? These are pertinent questions of practical importance for DAC countries.

The results of this study demonstrate that DAC trade is becoming increasingly regionalised as revealed by concentration ratios, trade shares and growth rates. Alongwith that, has increased openness to trade and trade with rest of the World. However, the same conclusion does not hold for agricultural products in which a geographic bias is found to have declined during 1994 to 2000.

This increased regionalisation of trade in DAC occurred despite the fact that there was no region wide regional trade agreement. Though there is a trading bloc at the sub regional level (ASEAN), its initiative to move towards free trade area (AFTA) has not brought a significantly higher reduction in tariff or other trade restrictions for its members during the

1990s compared to such reduction by other countries in the region. Despite this, regionalisation of trade has proceeded. The factors enabling this are briefly as follows: more open trade policy, reduced intra regional barriers and some similarity in the external trade policy followed by Asian countries. Pursuit of more outward oriented policies has been the major stimulus for increasing intra regional trade.

The trade pattern in DAC during the 1990s shows that the neighbourhood factor has encouraged trade and a policy of trade liberalisation has led to a growth in the share of intra regional trade. Referring to exactly this kind of pattern Diao *et al.* (2000) observe:

> *...if this pattern occurs, then neighbouring countries become more specialised. Regional trade arrangements may then be entered to further remove obstacles to trade and policy reversals"* p.5.

Based on a study of existing RTAs like the EU, NAFTA, MERCUSOR Diao *et al.*, conclude that the formation of these RTAs was preceded by faster growth rate in intra regional trade than extra regional trade and that it is natural to form RTAs when neighbourhood trade grows so as to harmonise policies and to remove other barriers.

It is ironical that the fast growth of intra regional trade in Asia has not been followed by any regional integration in the form of trade blocs. This is depriving Asia of a vast opportunity for trade creation and improvement in the welfare of Asian countries which is likely to have a positive effect on the welfare of other countries also. An important message from these findings is that the pattern of trade in DAC has strongly evolved towards the formation of RTAs. It is now for the governments in the region to take the initiative to forge a suitable regional trading arrangement for freer trade so that they can take advantage of the emerging opportunity in regional trade.

6

Main Findings and Suggestions for a Regional Strategic Framework for Trade in Asia

THE global trade environment has undergone profound changes during the decade of 1990s and the early years of twenty first century. The period was marked by the successful conclusion and implementation of the Uruguay round General Agreement on Trade and Tariff under the auspices of World Trade Organisation (WTO) to promote multi lateral trade. At the same time, the post WTO period has also witnessed a proliferation in regional and bilateral free trade agreements providing preferential access to the members and discriminating against others who are not members of the agreement. Apparently, this appears to be in confrontation with the WTO principle of most favoured nation treatment to all WTO members without any discrimination. However, GATT Article XXIV provides derogation from this principle. The Article allows regional trading arrangements as a special exception provided certain strict criteria are met. The Article states that if a free trade area or custom union is created, duties and other trade barriers should be reduced or removed on substantially all sectors of trade in the group. Non members should not find trade with the group more restrictive than before the group was set up. The post WTO period has seen countries rushing to reach preferential trading arrangements (PTAs) not only in their regional proximity but even with countries located at far off places and in different continents. In most of the cases several items are excluded from reduction in trade barriers with scant regard to the provisions of Article XXIV.

Initially, it appeared as if failure to successfully negotiate a multilateral trade agreement was leading to the emergence of regional groupings but subsequent events show that regionalism has grown very fast after the successful multilateral Uruguay round in 1994. This could be attributed to two reasons. One, that countries are trying to use PTAs as a safeguard against liberalisation mandated by the WTO agreement, and two, countries see a big advantage and feel more at ease in opening up trade with other suitable members than with a very large number of countries.

Serious concern is being expressed about the impact of growth in PTAs on multilateralism but there is no consensus on the likely impact of PTAs on multilateral trade liberalisation and in enhancing global welfare. Some researchers see PTAs as a stumbling block while others see them as a building block for multilateralism. Even though there is a stronger case in favour of a multilateral trade arrangement and against PTAs, it is difficult to restrain members to seek preferential trading arrangements on the ground that it would have an adverse impact globally. The present situation and global undercurrents indicate that the current wave of regionalism is going to stay for long.

This has serious implications for countries which have so far not opted for participation in any kind of PTA. As a PTA helps in trade promotion in general among the countries that constitute the trading group and also creates protection against outside members while liberalising on a selective basis, it put the other countries, not part of PTA, in a disadvantageous position in terms of access to markets of countries operating in a Preferential Trade Area *vis à vis* the countries within the PTA. Also, the countries not part of trading bloc are unable to go for selective liberalisation with some countries, if perceived to be beneficial, without allowing such liberalisation to all the countries. This causes strong externality for the countries which are not part of any PTA and becomes strong motivation for forming PTAs to counter the adverse impact of other PTAs. This is generally termed as external factor for formation of PTAs.

The current spate of regionalism has some strategic implications for forging regional trading arrangement in Asia. This is, that even if there is no conviction about positive role of trading blocs for global welfare there is a need for sort of Asian FTA to counter the adverse impact of PTAs cropping up at other places on Asian countries.

The second and more important motivation for forming regional trade agreement comes from the internal factors reflected in trade pattern among the countries in the region and growth in total and intra regional trade *vis à vis* growth in extra regional trade and in world trade. These patterns were studied separately for the group of Developing Asian Countries (DAC) and for Japan. DAC as a group has been showing economic dynamism in the recent years with a faster growth in GDP and trade. The GDP of DAC groups during 1991 to 2000 increased two and half times faster than the global economy and about five times faster than the Japanese economy. Similarly, DAC trade increased annually by 8.5 per cent compared to the 6.6 per cent growth rate in world trade and 4.3 per cent in Japanese trade. Also DAC exports were rising faster than DAC imports. These variations in growth rate in output and trade have caused a significant impact on the trade pattern among the DAC and with the outside world.

DAC trade showed a higher growth rate than world trade for both types of products namely agricultural and non-agricultural but there were some distinguishing features in the two types of trade. First, the difference in growth rates in DAC and world trade was much higher for non-agricultural trade than agricultural trade. Second, DAC trade in non-agricultural products showed almost double the growth rate shown by DAC agricultural trade during 1990 to 2000. Third, DAC export of non-agricultural products was increasing faster than imports whereas the reverse holds true for agricultural trade.

Dividing the export and import from developing Asian countries in intra and extra categories also shows strong patterns. The growth rate in intra DAC exports was about one percentage point higher than extra DAC export but import among DACs increased by more than double the rate of growth in DAC import from rest of the World. Faster growth in intra DAC import compared to extra DAC import is due to trade in non-agricultural products and agricultural products show a slightly lower growth in intra DAC imports compared to extra DAC import. In the case of exports, intra DAC trade in non-agricultural products was increasing only at a slightly higher rate than extra DAC trade but intra DAC export of agricultural products was increasing at more than double the growth rate in extra DAC exports. In other words, for non-agricultural products intra Asia imports were rising at a much faster rate than extra Asia imports and for agricultural products intra Asia exports were rising at a much faster rate than extra Asia exports. This shows that the demand for Asian products was expanding much faster in Asia than in the rest of the World.

In the case of Japan, its imports from Asia during 1991 to 2000 increased annually at the rate of 8 per cent, whereas imports from rest of the World witnessed a meagre 1.42 per cent growth. Similarly, Japan's export to Asian countries followed a growth rate of about 5 per cent compared to less than three per cent for rest of the World. In contrast to this, DAC import from Japan and export to Japan increased at a lower rate compared to imports from and exports to outside Asia.

An obvious consequence of the higher growth rate in Asia's trade compared to world trade is an increase in the share of Asia in world trade. Similarly, a higher growth rate in intra regional trade compared to extra regional trade implies changes in the regional concentration of trade. The share of DAC in the total world trade moved up sharply in the first half of 1990s but followed a small deterioration during the second half of 1990s. There are several reasons for a slowdown in Asia's share in world trade after showing a peak in the mid 1990s. The foremost reason is the Asian crisis. The second reason could be the emergence of RTAs in the world outside Asia in the post WTO period.

Total trade (import plus export) of Developing Asian Countries showed a continuous increase in regional concentration throughout the decade of 1990s. The increase in concentration of trade within the DAC group is observed for both agricultural as well as non-agricultural commodities. However, non-agricultural trade shows a much faster growth in regional concentration as compared to agricultural trade. Second, agricultural trade did not show an increase in concentration in DAC between TE 1995 and TE 2000.

Japan accounted for more than one fifth of the total merchandise import and offered a market for more than 13 per cent of the merchandise export of the DAC group during early 1990s. The share of Japan dropped by three percentage points in the case of imports and two percentage points in the case of exports. This decline is much bigger than the decline in the share of Japan in world trade. The main reason for this is that the growth rate in Japan's trade during 1990s could not keep pace with the growth rate in trade originating in other Asian countries. Despite these reversals in the Japan–DAC trade, Japan is a very big trading partner for DAC for agricultural exports and non-agricultural imports. For Japan, the importance of the group of Developing Asian Countries for trade purposes has increased during the 1990s whereas the importance of Japan for DAC has declined in the same period. Consequently, it turns out that the trade concentration of DAC trade with Japan declined during the 1990s in contrast to the considerable increase in trade concentration within the DAC group. The most important reason for this seems to be the growth rates of output in DAC and Japan.

In order to see whether changes in Asia's trade pattern resulted due to the changes in a few countries or were a larger phenomenon, the countrywise trade trends were also analysed for major Asian economies. The trade of each Asian country with group of DAC increased at a much faster rate than trade with rest of the World (ROW) during 1991-2000, except China and Cambodia whose trade grew faster with ROW. Accordingly, except China and Cambodia, the share of each country's trade going to DAC followed a substantial increase during the 1990s.

Bangladesh traded three fourth of goods with ROW during TE 1990 which came down to less than two thirds during TE 2000. The situation is almost similar for Sri Lanka. Ten years back Japan shared 70 per cent of its trade with ROW and 30 per cent with Asian developing countries. In the recent years the share of its trade with DAC increased to 39 per cent. Among all the Asian countries India transacted a minimum proportion (11.8%) of its merchandise trade with Developing Asian Countries during TE 1990. In next ten years it shared more than 24 per cent of its trade with DAC. The highest decline in trade share of the outside Asia region in a country's trade was observed in the case of Vietnam with its share falling from 74 per cent during TE 1990 to 32 per cent during TE 2000.

It is interesting to observe that all the Developing Asian Countries except Pakistan improved their share in world trade during 1990s which is evidence of their better trade performance compared to the rest of the World.

A higher growth rate in DAC trade compared to the rest of the World and a much higher growth in intra regional trade as compared to extra regional trade during 1990s, follow the implementation of trade liberalisation policies by DAC. This is reflected in the dismantling of trade barriers and reduction in the tariff rates on imports by almost all the countries. All the countries in DAC group lowered the tariff on imports during the 1990s. This liberalisation of tariff and the removal of trade restrictions is a significant factor for high growth in total DAC trade and a still higher growth rate in intra regional trade. These changes have been followed by a faster growth in intra Asia trade and in the share of Asia in world trade. Share of intra DAC trade in the world trade almost doubled between 1990 and 2000. There was also a substantial increase in the share of extra Asia trade in world trade during the early years of decade of 1990s after which it remained constant. This shows that the share of intra Asia trade did not increase at the cost of extra Asia trade. Second, the increased concentration of trade in DAC group followed from trade in non-agricultural products whereas there was no evidence of such a concentration in the case of agricultural trade after 1994.

The intensity index for extra regional and intra regional trade shows that Developing Asian Countries trade disproportionately more among themselves than with the rest of the World, indicating a strong regional bias in trade. Neighbourhood bias in trade was found in all the countries except India during the early 1990s. In the next ten years India also started trading at a disproportionately higher level with the Asian countries.

A strong neighbourhood bias was also found in the case of agricultural trade in DAC countries but it did not show any evidence of faster growth in intra DAC trade in most of the years during the 1990s. Nor there was any increase in the share of intra regional agricultural trade after 1994. Thus, increased regionalisation of DAC trade resulted from increased regionalisation of trade in non-agricultural products. The reason for agricultural trade not showing an increased regional concentration seems to be that even during the post WTO period DAC countries did not strongly follow the liberalisation of agricultural trade, and much less than liberalisation of non-agricultural trade.

Alongwith an increased regionalisation of trade, the policies followed by DAC during the decade of 1990s led to an increase in the proportion of GDP traded. The share of trade in GDP increased from 47.3 per cent during TE 1992 to 58.4 per cent during TE 2000. This raised the propensity to trade extra regionally from 0.349 to 0.409 during 1990 to 2000. This shows that fast growth in internal trade in the region has been accompanied by the tendency to trade more and more with the outside world. This has created trade opportunities outside DAC i.e. external trade creation. For the world as a whole trade creation has been stronger than trade diversion because of the increased regionalisation of DAC trade during the period

1990 to 2000. In other words, this can be taken to mean that regionalisation of trade in developing Asia during 1990s has improved welfare for developing Asia and for the rest of the World.

A strong neighbourhood bias in trade followed by further regionalisation and increased concentration and accompanied by trade creation and not trade diversion has clear implications of an enhancement of the benefit to countries in the region. This increased regionalisation of trade in DAC occurred despite the fact there was no region wide regional trade agreement. The factors behind this are more open trade policy, reduced intra regional barriers and some similarity in external trade policy followed by Asian countries. Pursuit of more outward oriented policies has been the major stimulus for increasing intra regional trade. The trade pattern in DAC during 1990s shows that neighbourhood factor has encouraged trade and that the policy of trade liberalisation has led to a growth in share of intra regional trade.

A combination of such favourable internal factors is a clear evidence of a large potential for further growth in trade which can be harnessed by harmonising policies and removing other barriers. Several studies show that this kind of evolution, as experienced in DAC during the 1990s, has been followed by the creation of regional trading blocs like the EU, NAFTA, MERCUSOR. It is thus natural to form RTA in Asia to take advantage of a favourable internal environment in the region.

It is ironical that fast growth of intra regional trade in Asia has not been followed by any regional integration in the form of trade blocs. This is depriving Asia of a vast opportunity for trade creation and improvement in the welfare of Asian countries which is likely to have a positive effect on the welfare of other countries also. An important message from these findings is that as the pattern of trade in DAC has strongly evolved towards the formation of RTAs, it is now for the governments in the region to take the initiative to forge a suitable regional trading arrangement for freer trade in the region to take advantage of the emerging opportunity in regional trade.

It is unfortunate that there is no serious move in Asia to form a strong and genuine free trade area covering the large region despite GATT and WTO rules being biased toward regional trade arrangements and despite the internal and external factors strongly favouring such a regional framework. There are several reasons for it. Historic attempts in this direction have been marred by strong opposition from USA. It is well known that after the Malaysian Prime Minister, Mahathir, proposed the formation of the East Asian Trade Block in 1990 it was met with strong protests from the USA in the form of the threat to Japan that it would invoke the super 301 if the latter went ahead with it. Circumstances have totally changed since then. Super 301 is challenged in the WTO as it is found WTO inconsistent. There is a complete reversal in the stand of USA towards regional integration. From being a strong opponent of regionalism till the early 1980s, the USA has turned to regionalism and formed the regional trading bloc, NAFTA in 1990. Since then, it is making an attempt to extend integration of America into a single market (FTAA) which was proposed to be completed by January 2005 covering 34 countries in north and south America. USA is also entering into global bilaterals with countries in other continents. Thus, US opposition to attempts for regional integration in Asia has lost its substance; it can't advocate that "regionalism is good for us not for you."

The second reason for the absence of Asian trading blocs seems to be Japan's ambivalence, which might be largely due to its geographic location, to go with Asia or with the Pacific in regional integration in trade. The economic dynamism of developing Asia and the trade patterns observed during 1990s shows that Japan's trade is growing faster with Developing Asia than with the rest of the World. This makes a stronger case for Japan to have PTA with Developing Asia. Third, while acknowledging the desirability for Asia-wide trade blocs it has been found to be an infeasible proposition by some experts. Asia's diversity, political circumstances and the limited success of such attempts in the past are cited as reasons for the success of an Asia-wide trading bloc (Panagariya 1994 and Panagariya *et al.,* 1996). These factors apply in almost all the regions but these have been exaggerated in the case of Asia. History and experience show that such factors have not prevented PTAs outside Asia. The on-going trend in continental regionalism in Europe, America and Africa shows that countries with similar and even more diversity are coming together for the purpose of trade. Experience shows that if sufficient gains are seen then countries cooperate and adjust policies to participate in a particular arrangement. For instance, China's non market economy was seen as inconsistent with having it in PTA in Asia but China has become a member of WTO. This also despite the fact that Taiwan is also a WTO member.

Almost all Asian countries are making attempts to opt for bilateral kind of free trade agreements. Japan has concluded an FTA with the Republic of Singapore which became effective on 30th November, 2002 and negotiations are going on to conclude FTAs with South Korea and Mexico (Ogita 2003). ASEAN is trying to expand its free trade area to cover more countries particularly China, Japan and Korea. Some of the ASEAN members are trying to negotiate bilaterals with other Asian countries. In south Asia, India and Sri Lanka have entered into an FTA, and, India is in the advance stages of negotiating an FTAs with Thailand and Singapore. All these moves are indicators of the mood in Asia to go for regional cooperation in trade. However, such bilateral agreements also create problems like trade deflection, trade conflicts and make the situation in the region complex. Region wide framework of free trade area would obliterate the need for bilaterals and would also offer more opportunities for trade creation.

The next question is what should be the shape of regional integration arrangement in Asia. Our study shows that internal factors, revealed by emerging trade pattern, favour a free trade bloc among DAC. The study also shows that Japan's trade with DAC has a strong regional bias which has further deepened during the 1990s. Thus, Japan also stands to benefit from free trade with DAC. However, DAC trade with Japan did not indicate much scope for expanding trade opportunities with trade liberalisation. This happened mainly due to stagnation in the Japanese economy during the study period (1990-2001); there are now signs of a revival of growth in the Japanese economy. There are other strong reasons for DAC to benefit from regional cooperation with Japan. Japan is the biggest trading partner for all the countries in developing Asia. It provides the market for one fifth of agricultural exports from DAC and meets the same amount of imports requirement of DAC for non-agricultural products. Japan is biggest importer of agricultural products in the world and its import are more than the total agricultural export from developing Asia to the rest of the World. Moreover, multi-lateral trade accords under the auspices of WTO would require countries like Japan to provide more market access to agricultural imports. This would benefit DAC from PTA with Japan. DAC also would benefit from the flow of Japanese investments following any PTA.

To conclude, the internal as well as external factors strongly favour regional integration for trade in Asia. This would improve welfare not only of the Asian countries but also of rest of the World. Second, it would counter the adverse impact of the explosion in the number of RTAs around the world and would provide a strategic framework to deal with the proliferation of PTAs. Three, powerful supra RTA in Asia would obliterate the need for bilateral and sub regional RTAs which are likely to create problems in terms of trade deflections, spaghetti bowl and preferential trade agreement with countries from outside region. Four, it would be a strategic move to respond to strong continental trade groupings already created or being shaped up around the globe. Such an arrangement should not be confined to East Asia alone or South Asia alone. It should rather cover Japan and the entire developing Asia upto the Indian sub continent. In the long run free trade area in Asia might lead to the end of regionalism in favour of multiliteralism.

7

POSTSCRIPT

Regional Trading Agreements and India

INDIA is a founder member of GATT and has strongly supported multilateral trading system. Till a few years ago India did not join any Regional Trade Agreement or Preferential Trading Agreement but country has played active and leading role in promoting regional economic cooperation and trade in south Asia. Concrete shape to this idea was given with the formation of South Asian Association for Regional Cooperation (SAARC) in 1985 involving seven countries namely Pakistan, Bangladesh, Nepal, Sri Lanka, Bhutan and Maldives besides India. A regional trading block among these members was formed in April 1993 with the signing of SAARC Preferential Trading Agreement (SAPTA) for giving preferential market access to the exports of the member countries in a limited way. These countries have moved further to achieve South Asia Free Trade Area (SAFTA), modalities of which are being finalised. The agreement provides for trade liberalisation programme under which (1) India, Pakistan and Sri Lanka would reduce their existing tariffs to 20 per cent within two years from the date when the agreement would come into force, (2) Other members of SAARC, all four of which are LDC would reduce their tariff to 30 per cent, and (3) Each country will maintain a sensitive list to protect the interest of domestic stakeholders. SAFTA is proposed to come into force from 1st January 2006.

Some important aspects of trade relations among south Asian countries deserve to be mentioned here. One, because of historical hostilities between India and Pakistan much progress could not be achieved in regional trade in South Asia despite efforts for promoting preferential trade. Pakistan has still not granted even MFN status to India. Two, due to porous border lot of unrecorded exchange of goods takes place among neighbouring countries in the region particularly between India and Nepal. Three, India's geographic location is crucial to promote liberalised trade in the region as this big country either has a common border or has best proximity to other countries in the region. Probably it is because of the last factor that trade between south Asian countries and India has grown faster than trade between any other two south Asian countries. It can be seen from Table 7.1 that trade of Bangladesh, Pakistan and Sri Lanka with India increased at a much faster rate than growth rate in their trade with Asia and world.

Barring a few agricultural products tariff rate for SAARC countries' import to India are either lower than standard rate of duty or zero. The exact status for agricultural products is shown in Table 7.2.

TABLE 7.1

Growth Rate in Inter Country Trade among South Asian Countries between TE 1990 & TE 2000

(% per annum)

Country	Bangladesh	India	Pakistan	Sri Lanka
Bangladesh	—	19.0	2.3	–6.0
India	**19.0**	—	**13.5**	**17.7**
Pakistan	2.3	13.5	—	1.2
Sri Lanka	–6.0	17.7	1.2	—
Asia	14.0	17.5	6.4	13.4
World	9.3	8.6	4.7	10.8

TABLE 7.2

Concession to Agricultural Imports from SAARC Countries to India

Chapters	Products	SAARC (SAPTA) Preferential Treatment
Chapter – 3	Fish and crustaceans, molluscs and other aquatic invertebrates.	50% of effective duty to LDC in SAPTA
Chapter – 4	Dairy produce; birds' eggs; natural honey; edible products products of animal origin, not elsewhere specified or included	Free for SAARC subject to rules of origin, Eggs and mack and puma
Chapter 7	Edible vegetables and certain roots and tubers	Free
Chapter – 8	Edible fruit and nuts; peel of citrus fruits or melons	Free
Chapter – 9	Coffee, tea, mate and spices	
Chapter – 10	Cereals	No Concession
Chapter – 11	Products of the milling industry; malt; starches; inulin; wheat gluten.	Free

Contd. ...

...Table 7.2 Contd. ...

Chapters	Products	SAARC (SAPTA) Preferential Treatment
Chapter – 12	Oil seeds and oleaginous fruits; miscellaneous grins, seeds and fruit; industrial or medicinal plants; straw and fodder.	10% concession on duty
Chapter – 15	Animal or vegetable fats and oil and their cleavage products; prepared edible fats; animal or vegetable waxes.	50% of effective duty to LDC in SAPTA
Chapter – 17	Sugars and sugar confectionery	50% of effective duty to LDC in SAPTA
Chapter – 24	Tobacco and manufactured tobacco substitutes	Free
Chapter – 52	Cotton	50% of effective duty to LDC in SAPTA

As mentioned earlier except in South Asia, India had not taken much interest in regional trade grouping till a few years ago. However, with proliferation of RTAs, PTAs and FTAs elsewhere, in the aftermath of WTO, India has been actively exploring possibilities of entering into preferential trading agreement with a large number of countries. It has already floated some PTAs and is in the process of negotiating some more such arrangements described below.

1. Framework Agreement on Comprehensive Economic Co-operation between the Association of South East Asian Nations (ASEAN) and India.
2. BIMST-EC FTA

3. India-Singapore Comprehensive Economic Cooperation Agreement (CECA)
4. Framework Agreement for establishing Free Trade between India and Thailand
5. India-Sri Lanka Bilateral Free Trade Area and the Proposal for Comprehensive Economic Partnership Agreement
6. Agreement on South Asian Free Trade Area (SAFTA)
7. India-Mercosur PTA
8. India-SACU (Southern African Customs Union) Framework Agreement Joint Study Group (JSG) with Mauritius
9. India-GCC Framework Agreement
10. Joint Study Group with China
11. Joint Study Group between India and Republic of Korea, and India and Japan
12. Brief on India-Egypt PTA
13. Bangkok Agreement
14. Global System of Trade Preferences (GSTP)

I. Framework Agreement on Comprehensive Economic Co-operation between the Association of South East Asian Nations (ASEAN) and India

A Framework Agreement on Comprehensive Economic Cooperation between the Association of South East Asian Nations (ASEAN) and India was signed by the Prime Minster of India and the Heads of Nation/Governments of

ASEAN members during the Second ASEAN – India Summit on 8th October, 2003 in Bali, Indonesia. The key elements of the Framework Agreement on Comprehensive Economic Cooperation between the Association of South East Asian Nations (ASEAN) and India cover FTA in Goods, Services and Investment, as well as areas of Economic Cooperation. The Agreement also provides for an Early Harvest Programme (EHP) which covers areas of Economic Cooperation and a common list of items for exchange of tariff concessions as a confidence building measure. The highlights of the Framework Agreement are:

(i) FTA in Goods

Ngotiations to commence from January, 2004 and to be concluded by 30th June, 2005. The tariff reductions will start from 1st January, 2006 and Most Favoured Nations (MFN) tariff rates to be gradually eliminated. While India will eliminate tariffs in 2011 for Brunei Darussalam, Cambodia, Lao PDR, Indonesia, Malaysia, Myanmar, Singapore, Thailand and Vietnam; Brunei Darussalam, Indonesia, Malaysia, Singapore and Thailand will eliminate in 2011 and new ASEAN Member States i.e. CLMV will eliminate in 2016 for India. India and Philippines will eliminate tariffs for each other on a reciprocal basis by 2016.

(ii) FTA in Services

Negotiations to commence in 2005 and concluded by 2007. The identification, liberalisation etc. of the sectors of services to be finalised for implementation subsequently.

(iii) FTA in Investments

Negotiations to commence in 2005 and concluded by 2007. The identification, liberalisation etc. of the sectors of investment to be finalised for implementation subsequently.

(iv) Areas of Economic Cooperation

Areas of economic cooperation to include trade facilitation measures; sectors of cooperation; and trade & investment promotion measures.

(v) Early Harvest Programme (EHP)

Based on the inter-Ministerial consultations and apex chambers of commerce, the items for EHP were finalised for exchange of concessions.

As per the current status the ASEAN-India TNC is undertaking negotiations to establish an ASEAN-India Regional Trade and Investment Area (RTIA) which includes a Free Trade Area in goods, services and investment as per timeframes prescribed in the Framework Agreement. The TNC has finalised the modalities for progressive tariff elimination for EHP items and is currently discussing the Rules of Origin.

II. BIMST-EC FTA

The initiative to establish Bangladesh-India-Sri Lanka-Thailand Economic Cooperation (BIST-EC) was taken by Thailand in 1994 to explore economic cooperation on a sub-regional basis involving contiguous countries of South East & South Asia grouped around the Bay of Bengal. Myanmar was admitted in December, 1997 and the initiative was renamed as BIMST-EC. The initiative involves three members of SAARC (India, Bangladesh and Sri Lanka) and two members of ASEAN (Thailand, Myanmar). BIMST-EC is visualised as a 'bridging link' between two major regional groupings i.e. ASEAN and SAARC. Member countries have constituted the Trade Negotiating Committee to carry forward the programme, as stipulated in the Framework Agreement. Thailand is the chair country for the TNC. The First TNC meeting was held in Bangkok on 7-8 September, 2004 where the TNC finalised its Terms of Reference.

III. India-Singapore Comprehensive Economic Cooperation Agreement (CECA)

As agreed during the visit of Prime Minister to Singapore in April, 2002, a Joint Study Group (JSG) for establishing a Comprehensive Economic Cooperation Agreement (CECA) between the two countries was set up on 8th April, 2002. The JSG submitted its report to the two Prime Ministers on 8th April, 2003. The JSG identified areas of increased economic engagement between the two countries and also recommended early launching of negotiations for a CECA to include a) A Free Trade Agreement, which would include, *inter-alia,* trade in goods and services and investment; b) A bilateral agreement on investment promotion, protection and cooperation; c) An improved Double Taxation Avoidance Agreement; d) A more liberal Air Services Agreement and Open Skies for Charter Flights; and e) A work programme of cooperation in a number of areas including health care, education, media, tourism and the creation.

The 10th round of negotiations was held in New Delhi from 18-20th October, 2004. The negotiations on CECA are targeted to be concluded soon.

IV. Framework Agreement for Establishing Free Trade between India and Thailand

Framework Agreement for establishing Free Trade Area between India and Thailand was signed by the Commerce Ministers of the two sides on 9th October, 2003 in Bangkok, Thailand. The key elements of the Framework Agreement cover FTA in Goods, Services and Investment, and Areas of Economic Cooperation. The Framework Agreement also provides for an Early Harvest Scheme (EHS) under which common items of export interest to the sides have been agreed for elimination of tariffs on a fast track basis. Negotiations for FTA in goods are in advance stage and expected to be concluded in next few months. It is proposed to establish Free Trade Area (zero duty imports) by 2010.

V. India-Sri Lanka Bilateral Free Trade Area and the Proposal for Comprehensive Economic Partnership Agreement

A Bilateral Free Trade Agreement was signed between the Prime Ministers of India and Sri Lanka in New Delhi on 28th December, 1998 and has been in operation since March, 2000. This was the first FTA India had signed by then. The Agreement seeks to establish a Free Trade Area (FTA) through elimination of tariffs in a phased manner. India would reduce tariffs to zero on 1350 tariff lines immediately on implementation of the Agreement. For the rest, except 429 items included in the Negative List, across the board duty free access would be given over a period of 3 years from the date of implementation of the Agreement. There is a tariff rate quota on tea for 15 million kgs. and on garments for 8 million pieces. From 18th March, 2003, India's commitment of duty reduction has been completed. The items in the Negative List of 429 tariff lines at 6 digit level of Harmonised Code are from various sectors like rubber and rubber products, paper and paper boards, plastics and products thereof, coconuts, alcoholic beverages and textile items, etc.

Sri Lanka would give 100 per cent duty concessions on 319 tariff lines on the date of operationalisation of the Agreement. In addition, it has given 50 per cent tariff concessions on 839 tariff lines on the date of operationalisation of the Agreement which has been deepened to 100 per cent as on today. For the remaining items, Sri Lanka would reduce tariffs to zero per cent over a period of 8 years in three phases i.e. by 35 per cent and 70 per cent & 100 per cent before the expiry of 3rd, 6th and 8th year respectively. In other words, India's exports on these items get 35 per cent duty concessions from Sri Lanka as on today. Sri Lanka's Negative List comprises of 1180 tariff lines.

The preferential trade under the FTA is governed by the Rules of Origin which specify three criteria namely: (i) the domestic value addition should be 35 per cent, (ii) inputs to undergo substantial transformation at 4-digit level of customs harmonised code, and (iii) a list of operations like simple packing, cutting and assembly etc. have been defined which would not qualify for duty free market access. If the raw material/inputs are sourced from one country by the other, the value addition is reduced to 25 per cent within the overall limit of 35 per cent.

Satisfied by the progress of expansion of trade made possible by the ISLFTA two countries are now exploring ways and means of deepening and widening economic cooperation through a Comprehensive Economic Partnership Agreement (CEPA).

VI. Agreement on South Asian Free Trade Area (SAFTA)

This Agreement shall supersede the Agreement on SAARC Preferential Trading Arrangement (SAPTA). SAFTA Agreement was signed during the 12th SAARC Summit held in Islamabad on 4-6th January, 2004. The Agreement provides for free trade in goods among SAARC member countries. Under this Non-LDC countries India, Pakistan and Sri Lanka would reduce their existing tariffs to 20 per cent within a time frame of two years from the date of coming into force of the Agreement. If the actual tariff rates are below 20 per cent then there shall be an annual reduction of 10 per cent on Margin of Preference basis for each of the two years. The subsequent tariff reductions from 20 per cent or below to 0-5 per cent shall be done within a period of five (for Sri Lanka it is six) years, beginning from the third year from the date of coming into force of the Agreement.

The LDC Member countries would reduce their existing tariff to 30 per cent within a time frame of two years from the date of coming into force of the Agreement. If actual tariff rates are below 30 per cent there will be an annual reduction of 5 per cent on Margin of Preference basis for each of the two years. The subsequent tariff reductions from 30 per cent or below to 0-5 per cent shall be done within a period of eight years, beginning from the third year from the date of coming into force of the Agreement.

Each country will maintain a sensitive list to protect the interests of the domestic stakeholders.

SAFTA agreement will enter into force on 1st January, 2006 upon completion of negotiations on Sensitive Lists, Rules of Origin, Revenue loss Compensation Mechanism for LDCs.

VII. India-Mercosur PTA

MERCOSUR is a trading block in Latin America comprising Brazil, Argentina, Uruguay and Paraguay as its members. It is the fourth largest integrated market after the European Union (EU), North American Free Trade Agreement (NAFTA) and ASEAN. It has 150 billion dollars of trade. India had a total trade of US$ 1247.32 million with MERCOSUR with approx. US$ 385.45 million as exports and US$ 861.87 million imports during 2003-2004. India's share is just 0.83 per cent of the global imports of MERCOSUR. India's major items of exports to MERCOSUR are drugs, pharmaceuticals and fine chemicals, transport equipment, inorganic/organic/agro chemicals, cotton yarn & fabric, made-ups, readymade garments, cotton & manmade yarn fabrics, dyes, intermediates and coal tar. The major imports into India from MERCOSUR are edible (vegetable) oils, metalliferous ores, metal scrap and non-electrical machinery.

A Framework Agreement on Preferential Trade Agreement (PTA) was signed in New Delhi on January 25, 2004, coinciding with the visit of the President of Brazil. The aim of this Preferential Trade Agreement is to expand and strengthen the existing relations between MERCOSUR and India, promote the expansion of trade by granting reciprocal tariff reductions and ultimately to create a free trade area between them.

VIII. India-SACU (Southern African Customs Union) Framework Agreement

South Africa along with Lesotho, Swaziland, Botswana and Namibia has formed the Southern African Customs Union (SACU) with a common custom tariff policy. South Africa and India are members of the Indian Ocean Rim Association for Regional Cooperation. South Africa is a member of the World Trade Organisation and has also finalised a free trade and development agreement with European, which provides for gradual liberalisation of the two way trade between South Africa and European Union. South Africa has also signed a Framework Agreement for the creation of a Free Trade Area with Southern Common Market (MERCOSUR).

A Joint Working Group was set up to initiate negotiations for a Comprehensive Framework Agreement between India and SACU. Text of the Framework Agreement was finalised in September, 2004. The Framework Agreement provides for a limited tariff concession in the first stage and later on graduating to a Free Trade Arrangement. The negotiations for PTA are to be completed by the end of December, 2005. There is no time frame for initiating the negotiations on FTA. The necessary mandate in this regard will be sought from the cabinet very shortly.

Serious efforts are on to work out to explore and work out modalities for Comprehensive Economic Coop and Partnership Agreement (CECPA) with Mauritius, gulf countries consisting of Bahrain, Kuwait, Oman, Qatar, Saudi Arabia and United Arab Emirates, China, Republic of Korea and Japan, Singapore and Egypt.

IX. Bangkok Agreement

The Bangkok Agreement is an initiative under the Economic and Social Commission for Asia and the Pacific (ESCAP) for trade expansion through exchange of tariff concessions among developing country members of the ESCAP region. This agreement was signed on 31st of July, 1975. Seven countries namely, Bangladesh, India, Lao PDR, Republic of Korea, Sri Lanka, the Philippines and Thailand met at Bangkok and agreed to a list of products for mutual tariff reduction. However, this agreement was not ratified by Thailand and the Philippines due to their ASEAN commitments, which was also coming into force at that time. This agreement remained operational between four countries namely, Bangladesh, India, Republic of Korea and Sri Lanka. The developing countries and associate members of ESCAP are eligible to accede to the Agreement. China is also a member of it now.

Three rounds of trade negotiations have been held. The First Round was in 1975 when the agreement was signed and the Second Round commenced in 1988 and was completed in 1990. Upto the Second Round, India's general concessions on 106 items correspond to 188 tariff lines (six-digit HS). The 12 items on which special concessions have been provided to Bangladesh correspond to 33 tariff lines. On China's accession to Bangkok Agreement, India has extended the concessions which it has already extended to other developing member countries of Bangkok Agreement, China has granted concessions on 217 items (ITC HS Code 8-digit) to India in addition to the concessions already granted to other member countries of the Agreement. These concessions have been made effective from 1st January, 2004.

The Third Round of Negotiations under the Bangkok Agreement was launched in October, 2001, and concluded recently. The exchange of concessions during the Third Round of Negotiations can be summarised in the following manner:

(i) No concessions were exchanged with Sri Lanka as India has already entered into a bilateral Free Trade Agreement with Sri Lanka.

(ii) As Bangladesh is the only Least Developed Country (LDC) member in the Bangkok Agreement, India agreed to extend unilateral tariff preferences to Bangladesh on 25 items based on the principle of non-reciprocity.

(iii) India gave concessions to China on 311 items (6-digit HS) and received concessions from China on 589 items (8-digit HS).

(iv) India gave concessions to Republic of Korea on 88 items (6-digit HS) and received concessions from Republic of Korea on 138 items (8-digit HS).

X. Global System of Trade Preferences (GSTP)

The Agreement establishing the Global System of Trade Preferences (GSTP) among Developing countries was signed on 13th April, 1988 at Belgrade following conclusion of the First Round of Negotiations. The Agreement entered into force on 19th April, 1989. Forty-four countries have ratified the Agreement and have become participants.

The GSTP establishes a framework for the exchange of trade concessions among the members of the Group of 77. The coverage of the GSTP extends to arrangements in the area of tariffs, para-tariff, non-tariff measures, direct trade measures including medium and long-term contracts and sectoral agreements. One of the basic principles of the Agreement is that it is to be negotiated step by step improved upon and extended in successive stages. During the First Round India exchanged concessions with 14 countries. The number of tariff lines on which concessions were granted by India is 31 and in return India received tariff concessions on a wide range of products of its export interest from these 14 countries.

In order to carry forward the exchange of concessions, the second round of GSTP Negotiations was launched in 1991. During the Second round, India held bilateral negotiations for exchange of concessions with 12 countries. These concessions have not been implemented so far. In the Special Ministerial Session of the Committee of Participants held in Sao Paulo during UNCTAD XI on 16th June, 2004, the Ministers decided to launch the third round of negotiations under the GSTP. As per the decision taken therein, a Negotiating Committee will commence negotiations in November, 2004 and conclude the negotiations by not later than November, 2006.

India so far has free trade bilateral agreements with Sri Lanka and Nepal but it is moving fast to establish FTAs with several other countries or group of countries.

Bibliography

Alesina, Alberto and Wacziarg, Romain (2000). "Economic Integration and Political Distintegration." *American Economic Review,* 90, 1276-96.

Anderson, Kym and Hege Norheim (1994). "Is World Trade Becoming More Regionalised," in Ross Garnaut and Peter Drysdale (ed.) *Asia Pacific Regionalism: Readings in International Economic Relations.* Harper Educational, pp. 125-142.

Axline, W. Andrew (1994). *The Political Economy of Regional Cooperation: Comparative Case Studies,* Fairleigh Dickinson University Press, Cranbury, NJ.

Bagwell, Kyle, and R.W. Staiger (1998). "Will Preferential Agreements Undermine the Multilateral Trading System?" *Economic Journal* 108 (July): 1162-82.

Bank of Kanas City, *Symposium on the Policy Implications of Trade and Currency Zones,* 7-42.

Bergsten, C. Fred (1996). "Globalising Free Trade." *Foreign Affairs,* 75, 105-20.

Bergstrand, Jeffrey H. (1985). "The Gravity Equation in International Trade: Some Microeconomic Foundations and Empirical Evidence." *Review of Economic and Statistics,* 67, 474-81.

Bhagwati, J. (1992). "Regionalism *vs.* Multilateralism," *The World Economy* 15(5): 535-556.

————. (1993). "Regionalism and Multilateralism: An Overview," in Jaime de Melo and Arvind Panagariya (ed.) *New Dimensions in Regional Integration.* Cambridge University Press, pp.22-51.

Bhagwati, Jagdish and Arvind Panagariya (1996). "Preferential Trading Areas and Multilateralism- Strangers, Friends or Foes?" in J. Bhagwati and A. Panagariya, eds., *The Economics of Preferential Trade Agreements.* Washington, D.C.: American Enterprise Institute Press.

Bond, Eric W., and Constraintinos Syropoulos (1996a). "The Size of Trading Blocs: Market Power and World Welfare Effects." *Journal of International Economics*: 40(May): 411-37.

Carnoy, Martin (1970). "A Welfare Analysis of Latin American Economic Union: Six Industry Studies." *Journal of Political Economy,* 78, 626-54.

Casella, Alessandra (1995). "Large Countries, Small Countries and the Enlargement of Trade Bloc." *Working Paper 5365,* National Bureau of Economic Research, Cambridge, Mass.

Chang, Won and L. Alan Winters (1999). "How Regional Blocs Affects Excluded Countries: The Price Effects of MERCOSUR." *Discussion Paper Series No., 2179.* Centre for Economic Policy Research, London.

Collier, Paul (1979). "The Welfare Effects of Customs Unions: An Anatomy." *Economic Journal,* 89, 84–95.

De Janvry, Alain, Sadoulet, Elizabeth, and Gordillo de Anda, Gustavo (1995). "NAFTA and Mexico's Maize Producers." *World Development,* 23, 1349-62.

De la Torre, Augusto and Kelly, Margaret (1992). "Regional Trade Arrangements." *IMF Occasional Paper No. 93.* Washington DC.

dell'Aquila, Crescenzo, Rakhal Sarker, and Karl D. Meilke (1999). "Regionalism and Trade in Agrifood Products," *Working Paper 99-5,* International Agricultural Trade Research Consortium, University of Minnesota, St.Paul, Minnesota, USA.

Delle-Donne and Rodrik, Dani (1993). "The New Regionalism: A Country Perspective." in Jaime de Melo and Arvind Panagariya (eds.), *New Dimensions in Regional Integration. Cambridge University Press*, 159-93.

Diao, Xinshen, Terry Roe and Agpi Somwaru (1999). "What is the Cause of Growth in Regional Trade: Trade Liberalization or RTA's?" *Working Paper 99-1.* International Agricultural Trade Research Consortium, University of Minnesota, St.Paul, Minnesota, USA.

Erzan, Refik, and Yeats, Alexander (1992). "Free Trade Agreements with the United States: What's in it for Latin America?" *World Bank ORE Working Paper No. 827.* Washington DC.

Ethier, Wilfred (1998). "Regionalism in a Multilateral World." *Journal of Political Economy,* 106, 1214-45.

Ethier, Wilfred J. (1998). "The New Regionalism." *The Economic Journal*, 108 July.

Foreouton Faceh (1998). "Does Membership of a Regional Preferential Trade Arrangement Make a Country More or Less Protectionist?" *The World Economy* 21: 305-36.

Foroutan, Faezeh (1993). "Regional Integration in Sub-Saharan Africa: Past Experience and Future Prospects." in Jaime de Melo and Arvind Panagariya (eds.), *New Dimensions in Regional Integration.* Cambridge University Press, 234-71.

Frankel Jeffrey (1993). "Is Japan creating a Yen Bloc in Asia and the Pacific?" in Jeffrey Frankel and Miles Kahler (eds.), *Regionalism and Rivalry: Japan and the United States in Pacific Asia.* University of Chicago Press, 53-85; reprinted in Garnaut and Drysdale (1994,11-19).

Frankel, J.E. Stern and S. Wei (1996). "Regional Trading Arrangements: Natural or Super-Natural?" *American Economics Review* 86(2): 52-56.

Frankel, Jeffrey (1997). *Regional Trading Blocs in the World Economic System.* Washington, D.C.: Institute for International Economics.

Garnaut, Ross and Peter Drysdale (ed). *Asia Pacific Regionalism: Readings in International Economic Relations*, Harper Educational.

Garnaut, Ross, and Drysdale, Peter (eds.) (1994). *Asia Pacific Regionalism: Readings in International Economic Relations.* Pymble, NSW: HarperCollins.

Gross, G., and E. Helpman (1994). "Protection for Sale." *American Economic Review* 84(4): 833-50.

Grossman Gene and Krueger, Alan (1993). "Environmental Impacts of a North American Free Trade Area." in Peter M. Garber (ed.), *The Mexico-USA Free Trade Agreement. Free Trade Agreement.* Cambridge, Mass: Mit Press, 13-56.

Grossman (1995). "The Politics of Free-Trade Agreements." *American Economic Review* 85(4):667-90.

Haaland, Jan (1990). "Assessing the Effects of EC Integration on EFTA Countries: The Position of Norway and Sweden." *Journal of Common Market Studies* 28, 379-400.

Haimilton, Bob, and Whalley, John (1985). "Geographically Discriminatory Trade Arrangements." *Review of Economics and Statistics*, 67, 446 -55.

Hellvin, Lisbeth (1994). "Trade and Specialisation in Asia," *Lund Economic Studies No. 56.*

Holzman, Fraanklyn D. (1985). "Comecon: A Trade-Destroying Customs Union?" *Journal of Comparative Economics,* 9, 410-23.

Imada, Pearl (1993). "Production and Trade Effects of the Asean Free Trade Area." *The Developing Economies,* 31, 3-23.

Johnson, Harry G. (1965). "An Economic Theory of Protectionism, Tariff Bargaining and the Formation of Customs Unions." *Journal of Political Economy,* 73, 256-83.

————. (1970). "The Efficiency and Welfare Implications of the International Corporation." in Ian A. McDougall and Richard H. Snape (eds.), *Studies in International Economics.* Amsterdam : North-Holland, 83-103.

Ju, Jiandong, and Krishna, Kala (1996). "Market Access and Welfare effects of Free Trade Areas without Rules of Origin." *National Bureau of Economic Research Working Paper 5480,* Cambridge, Mass.

Kehoe, Patrick, and Kahoe, Timothy (1995). *Modellling North American Economic Integration.* Dordrecht: Kluwer.

Khan, S.M. and Z.S. Khan (2003). "Asian Economic Integration: A Perspective on South Asia," *Journal of Asian Economics*, 13.

Kirman, Alan P. (1973). "Trade Diverting Customs Unions and Welfare Improvement: A Comment." *Economic Journal*, 83, 459-80.

Koichi, Ohno (1993). *Regional Integration and Its Impact on Developing Countries.* Institute of Developing Economies, Tokyo, Japan.

Kojima, K. (1964). "The Pattern of International Trade Among Advanced Countries," *Hitotsubashi Journal of Economics* 5(1).

Kreinin, Mordechai E. (1994). "'Natural' Economic Blocs: An Alternative Formulation." *International Trade Journal*, 8, 193-205.

Krishna, Kala, and Krueger, Anno O. (1995). "Implementing Free Trade Areas: Rules of Origin and Hidden Protection" in Alan Deardorff, James Levionsohn and Robert Stern (eds.), *New Directions in Trade Theory*. Ann Arbor: University of Michigan Press, 149-87.

Krishna, Pravin (1998). "Regionalism and Multilateralism: A Political Economy Approach." *Quarterly Journal of Economics*, 113, 227-51.

Krueger, Anne O. (1997). "Free Trade Agreements *Versus* Customs Union." *Journal of Development Economics* 54: 169-87.

Krugman, Paul (1991). "Move Towards Free Trade Zones," Federal Reserve Bank of Kansa City *Economic Review* (Nov-Dec): 5-25.

————. (1991a). *Geography and Trade, Cambridge,* Mass: MIT Press.

————. (1991b). "The Move Towards Free Trade Zones." in Federal Reserve

————. (1991c). "The Move Towards Free Trade Zones." in Federal Reserve Bank of Kanas City, *Symposium on the Policy Implications of Trade and Currency Zones,* 7-42

————. (1991b). "Is Bilateralism Bad?" in El hanan Helpman and Assaf Razin (eds.), *International Trade and Trade Policy.* Cambridge, Mass.: MIT Press, 9-23.

————. (1993). "Regionalism *Versus* Multilateralism: Analytical Notes." in Jaime de Melo and Arvind Panagariya, Eds., *New Dimensions in Regional Integration.*

Lawrence, Robert Z. (1991). "Emerging Regional Arrangements: Building Blocks of Stumbling Blocks?" in R. O'Brien (Series ed.), *Finance and the Internationals Economy,* No 5. Oxford University Press for American Express.

Lloyd, Peter J. (1992). "Regionalisation and World Trade." *OECD Economic Studies*, 18, 7-43.

————. (1996). "The Changing Nature of Regional Trading Arrangements" in Bijit Bora and Christopher Findlay (eds.). *Regional Integration and the Asia-Pacific*. Melborune: Oxford University Press, 25-48.

Lortie, Pierre (1975). *Economic Integration and the Law of GATT.* New York: Praeger.

Lustig, Nora, Bosworth, Barry P., and Lawrence, Rzobert Z. (1992). *North American Free Trade: Assessing the Impact.* Washington DC: Brookings Institution.

Mayes, David G. (1978). "The Effects of Economic Integration on Trade." *Journal of Common Market Studies,* 17, 1-25.

McMillan, John (1993). "Does Regional Integration Foster Open Trade? Economic Theory and GATT Article XXIV" in Kym Anderson and Richard Blackhurst (eds.), *Regional Integration and the Global Trading System.* Hamel Hempstead (UK): Harvester Wheat Sheaf, 292-309.

Melo, Jaime de, Arvind Panagariya, and Dani Rodrik (1993). "The New Regionalism: A Country Perspective" in Jaime de Meloi and Arvind Panagariya, eds., *New Dimensions in Regional Integration.* New York and Melbourne: Cambridge University Press.

Michaely, Michael (1976). "The Assumption of Jacob Vine's Theory of Customs Union." *Journal of International Economics,* 6, 75-93

OECD (1993). *Regional Integration and Developing Countries,* Paris.

Ogita, Tatsushi (2003). "Japan as a Late Coming FTA Holder: Trade Policy Change for the Asian Orientation?" in Okamoto Jiro (ed.) *Whither Free Trade Agreements? Proliferation, Evaluation and Multilateralization,* IDE Development Perspective Series No. 2, IDE, JETRO, Chiba Shi, Japan.

Panagariya, Arvind (1994). "East Asia and New Regionalism," *World Economy,* 17(6).

———. (1995). *The Free Trade Area of the Americas: Good for Latin America?* Centre for International Economics, University of Maryland, Mimeo.

———. (1999). "Regionalism in Trade Policy : Essays on Preferential Trading," *World Scientific,* Singapore.

———. (2000). "Preferential Trade Liberalisation: The Traditional Theory and New Developments." *Journal of Economic Literature,* 38, 287-331.

Panagariya, Arvind and Ronald Findlay (1994). "A Political Economic Analysis of Free Trade Areas and Customs Unions." *Policy Research Working Paper No. 1261,* World Bank, Washington, D.C.

Panagariya, Arvind, M.G. Quibria and Narhari Rao (1996). "The Emerging Global Trade Environment and Developing Asia," *Economic Staff Paper Number 55,* Asian Development Bank, Manila.

Panagariya Arvind and T.N. Srinivasan (1998). "The New Regionalism; a Benign or Malign Growth," in Jagdish Bhagwati and Mathiahs Hirsch ed. *The Uruguay Round and Beyond Essays in Honour of Arthur Dunkel,* Springer–Verlag, p.221.

Park, Jee-Hyeong (2000). "International Trade Agreements between Countries of Asymmetric Size." *Journal of International Economics,* 50, 473-95.

Petri, Peter (1993). "The East Asian Trading Bloc: An Analytical History" in Jeffrey Franke l and Miles Kahler (eds.), *Regionalism and Rivalry,* University of Chicago Press, 21-52.

Pomfret Richard (2001). *The Economics of Regional Trading Agreements*, Oxford University Press, Oxford.

Preeg, Ernest H. (1995). *Traders in a Brave New World: The Uruguay Round and the Future of the International Future System.* University of Chicago Press.

Robson, Peter (1983). *Integration, Development and Equity: Economic Integration in West Africa.* London: George Allen and Unwin.

————. (1984). *The Economics of International Integration,* 2nd edn. London: George Allen and Unwin.

————. (2000). "Review of The Economic of Regional Trading Arrangements." *Economic Journal,* 110, F767-70.

Rodrik, Dani (2000). "How far will International Economic Integration Go?" *Journal of Economic Perspectives*, 14, 177-86.

Salvitore, Dominick (1990). *International Economics*, Third Ed. Macmillan Publishing Company, New York.

Viner, Jacob (1950). *The Customs Union Issue.* Washington, D.C.: Carnegie Endowment for International Peace.

Whalley, John (1985). *Trade Liberalisation Among Major World Trading Areas.* Cambridge, Mass: Mit Press.

————. (1996). "Why Do Countries Seek Regional Trade Agreements?" in J. Frankel, ed., *The Rationalisation of the World Economy.* Chicago: Chicago University Press.

Wilmore, Larry (1976). "Trade Creation, Trade Diversion, and Effective Protection in the Central American Common Market." *Journal of Development Studies* 12:396-414.

Winters, L. Alan (1996a). "Regionalism and the Rest of the World." *CEPR Discussion Paper 1315,* Centre for Economic Policy Research, London.

Index

A

trading bloc, a 83
work programme of cooperation 108
health care, education, media, creation 108
Afghanistan 33
AFTA 19, 83
agricultural exports from DAC 42
agricultural imports 36
agricultural products 40
agricultural trade 45, 71, 77, 80
agricultural trade in DAC countries 79
air services agreement 108
Anderson, Kym 26
areas of economic cooperation 107
article V 17
article XXIV 17, 87, 88
ASEAN 83, 99, 104, 105, 112
ASEAN agreement in South East 19
ASEAN-India regional trade and investment area 107
Asia 33, 41
asia region 66
asia-wide trading bloc 98
asian countries 25, 49, 54, 60, 80, 83, 84
asian crisis 44, 92
asian developing countries 64
asian trading bloc 19, 98
asia's trade 42

B

Bahrain 114
Bangkok 108
Bangkok Agreement 105, 114, 115
Bangladesh 33, 51, 52, 58, 59, 63, 66, 69, 93
barriers 17
Bay of Bengal 107
Belgrade 116
Bhagwati, J. 15, 18, 20
bilateral agreement 99, 108
bilateral free trade agreement 109
bilateral trade 20
BIMST-EC 108
BIMST-EC FTA 104, 107

C

Cambodia 33, 59, 60, 62, 93
CECA 105, 108
CECPA 114
China 34, 51, 52, 54, 59, 62, 64, 93, 99, 114
 China–Vietnam trade 51
 China's non market economy 98
 China's trade with Asian countries 58
CLMV 106
concentration of trade 92, 94
concentration ratios 83
continental regionalism 98
countries in DAC group 94
countrywise growth rates 61
custom union 17

D

DAC 34, 42, 62
 group 46, 52, 80
 imports 40
 imports of non-agricultural products 46
 markets 63
 trade 38
Deardorf 20
developing Asia 25
developing asian countries 23, 25, 40, 42, 47, 51, 61, 67, 77, 92, 93, 94
Diao, Xinshen 20, 26, 67, 84
dimensions of trade 49
dismantling of trade barriers 94
diversity 49
double taxation avoidance agreement 108

E

early harvest programme (EHP) 106, 107
early harvest scheme 109
east asian trade block 97
economic globalism 16
economic growth 33
economic recession 54
economic stagnation 41
economies in Asia 49
Engel 20
ESCAP 114
Ethier, Wilfred 16
EU 96
ex-ante approach 21
external trade policy 96
extra Asia 44
 trade 71, 94
extra DAC import 40, 91
extra DAC trade in world trade 76
extra regional exports 77
extra regional trade 26, 91

F

food security 19
food shortages 19
Frankel, Jeffrey 20
free trade bloc among DAC 99
FTA 99
 in goods 106
 in investments 107
 in services 106

G

GATT 17, 19, 87, 97, 101
GDP 33
global bilaterals 98

global competitive liberalisation 14
global economy 33, 34
global GDP 34
global system of trade preferences (GSTP) 116
global trade environment 87
global welfare 18, 88
group of developing asian countries (DAC) 90
growth in Asia's export 76
growth path 76, 77
growth rate in GDP 34
growth rate in world trade 72
growth rate of trade 46
growth rates 83
    growth rates in inter country trade 51, 59
    growth rates in Japan's trade 41
GSTP 105, 117

H

harmonised code 110
Hongkong 33, 63, 64

I

India 19, 34, 52, 54, 66, 69, 93, 99
Indo-China trade 58
Indonesia 54, 58, 61, 64, 66
intensity index 77, 94
index of intensity to trade (IIT), changes in 78
inter country trade 49, 54, 57
inter regional trade 21
inter-alia 108
intra 26, 77
    intra Asia 44
    intra Asia imports 72
    intra Asia trade 22, 41, 69, 70, 71
    intra DAC imports 91
    intra DAC trade 36, 40, 94
    intra regional growth 26
    intra regional trade 21, 45, 82, 84, 91, 96

J

Japan 25, 33, 34, 41, 52, 57, 59, 99
    Japan–China trade 57
    Japanese economy 99
    Japan's export to DAC 36
    Japan's trade with DAC 47

K

Khan, S.M. 16
Khan, Z.S. 16
Korea 51, 52, 54, 58, 61, 99
Krugman, Paul 19, 21, 68
Kuwait 114

L

laggard Asian economies 34
Lao Vietnam 33
larger regional trade group 14
Latin America 112
liberalisation 14, 67
    liberalisation of agricultural trade 80, 95
    liberalisation of tariff 69

M

Mahathir 97
Malaysia 33, 51, 58, 59, 61, 64
margin of preference basis 112
market access 15, 100
Mauritius 114

merchandise imports 71
merchandise trade 51
MERCOSUR 96, 112, 113
Most Favoured Nations 106
  MFN clause 17
multi lateral trade 87, 100
  agreements 15
  multi-lateral Uruguay 13
  multilateral liberalisation 18
  multilateral trade liberalisation 14, 88
  multilateral trading system 101
  multilateral Uruguay round 16, 88
  multilateralism 14, 15, 16, 18, 100
Myanmar 33, 63

N

NAFTA 96, 97, 112
negative list 110
negotiations for FTA 109
neighbourhood 82, 95
  neighbourhood factor 96
  neighbourhood trade 20, 80
Nepal 33, 61, 63
new ASEAN member states 106
non-agricultural products 40, 94
non-agricultural trade 22, 45, 92
non-agriculture imports 36
Norheim, Hege 26

O

OECD 1993 15
Oman 114
open skies 108
open trade policy 96
openness to trade 80
other Asia 25

P

Pakistan 19, 51, 52, 54, 58, 59, 61, 64, 66, 69, 94
Panagariya, Arvind 17, 20, 98
partial liberalisation 17
per capita income 34
per capita income in DAC 34
Philippines 33, 51, 52, 54, 58, 59, 61, 69
political conflicts 19
position of DAC vis à vis World and Japan 34
post WTO period 17, 87, 88
poverty line 33
preferential trade area 14
preferential trade blocs 14
preferential trading agreement 14, 17
preferential treatment 21
propensity to export 31
propensity to import 31
propensity to trade 30, 80, 81, 82
PTAs 18

Q

Qatar 114

R

rationalisation 15
reduction in the tariff 94
regional bias 80
  in trade 77
regional concentration 44, 45, 76, 77, 82, 92
  regional concentration (bias) in trade 71, 78, 82, 91
regional cooperation in trade 99
regional economic cooperation 101
regional imports 76
regional integration 23

arrangement 99
for trade 100
regional integration in Asia 21
regional or preferential trade agreements 15
regional trade 23, 85
regional trade agreements 19, 21, 67, 68, 89
regional trade in Asia 41
regional trading 101
regional trading arrangement (RTA) 13, 16, 23, 44, 84, 85
regional trading bloc in Asia 18
regionalisation 26
regionalisation of trade 83, 84, 95, 96
regionalism 14, 15, 18, 89, 100
removal of trade restrictions 69
Republic of Korea 114
Roe, Terry 20, 26, 67
Rogers 20
rules of origin 110

S

SAARC 19, 101, 102
SAARC agreement in South Asia 19
SAFTA 101, 102, 105, 111
SAFTA agreement 112
Salvitore, Dominick 21, 68
SAPTA 111
Saudi Arabia 114
sensitive list 112
share of Asia in world trade 69
share of DAC in world trade 43
share of trade 62
share of trade in GDP 82
Singapore 33, 51, 54, 58, 59, 61
slowdown in Asia's share in world trade 44
socio cultural aspects 49
Somwaru, Agpi 20, 26, 67
south Asia 99, 104
south asian free trade agreement (SAFTA) 19
specialisation 15
Sri Lanka 51, 52, 63, 66, 93, 99, 110
Sri Lanka's trade 59
Srinivasan, T.N. 17
Stern, J.E. 20
surplus in trade balance 36

T

tariff barriers 17
Thailand 33, 51, 58, 59, 61, 69
The growth paths of DAC 76
intra, extra, total 76
total import by DAC 36
total regional imports 72
total trade of Japan 51
total world trade 91
trade barriers 18, 88
trade concentration 48, 77, 93
trade creation 83
trade diversion 83
trade intensity index 82
intra regional import 28
intra regional export 28
extra regional import 29
extra regional export 29
trade led growth 33
trade liberalisation 18, 21, 22, 49, 54
trade pattern 35
trade growth, patterns in 67
trade pattern in DAC 84
trade, rates of growth in 61
trade with Asia 62

trading blocs 13, 89
trend growth rate in GDP in DAC economies 34

U

UNCTAD 25, 117
United Arab Emirates 114
Uruguay Round Agreement (URA) 68

V

Vietnam 51, 54, 57, 58, 61, 63, 64, 66, 93

W

Wei, S. 20
World Bank 25
world development indicators 25
world export 42
world import 42
world population 34
world trade 42, 77, 92, 94
 world trade in agricultural products 38
WTO 13, 14, 19, 44, 87, 97